DELIGHTFUL TOFU COOKING

by Eng Tie Ang

D1279675

Published by:

AMBROSIA PUBLICATIONS

Seattle, Washington

Ambrosia Publications
P.O. Box 30818
Seattle, WA 98103
Phone (206) 789-3693
Fax   (206) 789-3693

Art Direction by: Eng Tie Ang
Cover Design by: Kate Rose
Cover Production by: Shawn Wheeler
Cover Photo by: Terry Pagos Photography
Design and Illustrations by: Eng Tie Ang
Food Styling by: Veleda Furtado and Joan Deccio Wickham
Food Styling Assistance by: Eng Tie Ang and Carla Ferreira
Editorial Direction by: Donald R. Bissonnette
Typography and Production by: Janusz Mydlarczyk
Published by: Ambrosia Publications - Seattle, Washington
Printed by: Publishers Press - Salt Lake City, Utah

Printed in the United States of America
First Edition
First Printing - 1996

ISBN: 0-9627810-1-0
Library of Congress Catalog Number: 96-85089

Dedication

Dedicated to Alex Chi Ang Bissonnette and André Chun Chi Ang Bissonnette, my lovely sons, for all the joy they bring me and for all the joy eating tofu will bring them in their lives.

On The Cover

Table of Contents

Acknowledgements

I would like to thank many people for their help, support, and encouragement in putting this book together. First, I would like to thank those who helped in the editing process: Debbie Turner, Sara Baldwin, and my husband, Donald R. Bissonnette. I especially owe these people my gratitude for the arduous task of debugging my manuscript and suggesting changes. Second, for giving me suggestions and generously allowing me to use various items for the cover photo, I would like to express my appreciation to: Malgorzata Mydlarczyk, Veleda Furtado, Lisa Sassi, Judi Hurley, Lynn Tungseth, Christina Taran, Rieko Tsukagoshi, Paula Hanna, Darlene Burt, and Tilden. Third, for moral and technical support, I would like to thank: my mother, Kang Siu Tjen, my father, Ang Bun Pit, Ang Sen Hoo, Paul Marcius Ang, Ang Sen Long, Rosanne Riley, Carl Bissonnette, Gerald Zampa, Kristen Smith, Chi Thi Pham, Lynn Smith, David Keene, Richard Middlebrook, Mary Lou Thompson, Libby Bowman, Hanifa Yahiaoui, Lourdes Romao, Rose Rentz, Carla Ferreira, Ramona Delgado, and Janusz Mydlarczyk. Fourth, I would like to thank my husband and two sons, Alex and André, for giving me their opinions on the recipes after eating tofu dishes very regularly over the months that I spent perfecting the recipes. Finally, I would like to thank all my cooking class students and friends for encouraging me to undertake this project. To all of the above, I offer my sincere thanks and gratitude.

Eng Tie Ang

Eng Tie Ang

Introduction

"Tofu. Isn't that that soft, white, cubed stuff that you get in Chinese restaurants?" asked Uncle Carl. Well, Uncle Carl was not really wrong, but he was only partially right, too. Tofu can be soft, medium, firm, or extra firm; cubed, mashed, sliced, or puréed; boiled, fried, barbecued, baked, or broiled; Chinese, Japanese, Vietnamese, Korean, or vegetarian. Increasingly, especially since the 1960s, it is also found in health-conscious homes and restaurants as a substitute for meat, eggs, or dairy products in many traditional recipes. For example, tofu burgers, tofu meat loaf, tofu crab dip, tofu cheese cake, tofu yogurt cake, soy bean milk, and tofu lasagna are just a few of the many possibilities of Western dishes that can use tofu as a healthful addition.

What exactly is tofu? Quite simply, it is the final product one gets after soaking fresh soy beans, grinding and then boiling the puréed beans, straining and curdling the resulting soy milk, and ladling the milk into forming boxes until it is firm. Or for most people, it is the packaged stuff we buy in markets. Either way, it is perhaps the only very healthy, nutritious, inexpensive, almost flavorless, cholesterol free product, high in vitamins, protein, and minerals while low in saturated fats, sodium, and calories. Also, because of its amazing ability to take on the flavor of whatever it is cooked with or marinated in, it is the perfect food for people who want delicious yet healthy meals or who have dietary constraints yet crave certain dishes that would otherwise be impossible to have. In a way, it is God's gift to both gourmets and gourmands who want to eat their favorite dishes while maintaining a healthy diet. Though tofu is a relatively recent introduction to the U.S. diet, it has been used in the Orient for over 2000 years. Quite naturally, there are probably thousands of traditional tofu recipes from the Orient, some of which are included in this book. However, my goal was to present my readers with alternative uses of tofu incorporated in Western recipes so that when preparing meals, they would not necessarily have to change their menus, just their method of preparation of their favorite dishes. Tofu, by its nature, only alters the nutritional value of a dish, not its flavor.

These recipes are designed to be both quick and easy, while maintaining their delicious appeal. Quick, easy, and healthy food does not have to be boring. By the careful blending of herbs, spices, and tofu, I have taken my cultural/ethnic background and knowledge of traditional Oriental cooking and combined it with my acquired knowledge of Western cooking (from having grown up in South America and lived in North America for the last 16 years). From this rather interesting base, I have been able to combine these two cooking traditions, incorporating tofu into Western dishes with the result being both pleasingly delicious and healthy.

There are some basic tips that will help the novice user of tofu which I'd like to share with you. As previously mentioned, all types of tofu are excellent sources of protein; however, the firmer the tofu, the greater the content of protein. Also, the firmer the tofu, the easier it is to slice and cube. Conversely, the softer the tofu, the better it is for mashing and puréeing. Another important tip to keep in mind when purchasing tofu is always try to get the freshest block possible. Tofu can keep for about two weeks refrigerated and vacuum packed. If it's not vacuum packed, be sure to rinse it off daily and change the water it is soaked in. If tofu starts to smell, turn color, or get slimy, throw it out. For marinating dishes with tofu, it is best to do so in the refrigerator for at least an hour so that the flavors have time to seep into the tofu. And keep in mind that tofu can be frozen and kept for a couple of months; however, its texture, flavor, and color will change: it will become firmer and chewy; it will have a smoky-bean taste; and it will become tan in color. Nutritionally, however, it will not change.

It has been my hope in writing this book to further the use of tofu in the West in order for people to continue enjoying their favorite dishes while maintaining a more healthy and nutritious diet. Remember that for thousands of years tofu has been known as a health food throughout the Orient; it's only been known for about 30 years in the West. With this book and others like it, this magical health product from the East that is so very good for the health can gain a wider acceptance in the West with the rapidly growing number of health and diet conscious people. My desire is that you and your family and friends savor the dishes in this book and experience the epicurean delights that await you.

About the Author

Eng Tie Ang was born in Indonesia of Chinese parents, moved to Brazil at the age of five, and came to the United States at the age of twenty-five. She learned cooking at an early age at home and in her parents' small restaurant in Suzano, Sao Paulo, Brazil. Her first and most influential cooking teacher was her mother, a master of various kinds of Oriental cooking. As a teenager, she studied Western cooking at a cooking school in her hometown. In addition to **Delightful Tofu Cooking**, she has published three other cookbooks: **Delightful Thai Cooking**, **Delightful Brazilian Cooking**, and **Delightful Vietnamese Cooking**. **Delightful Chinese Cooking**, **Delightful Indonesian Cooking**, and **Delightful Italian Cooking** are forthcoming. Another title to her credit is a children's cultural book entitled, **The Chinese Lantern Festival**. Ms. Ang is also a frequent contributor of recipes and other food related tips and advice to newspapers and magazines both in America and Brazil.

In addition to writing cookbooks, Ms. Ang has been a cooking instructor for the University of Washington's Experimental College. She also frequently teaches courses through the Puget Consumers' Co-op and other cooking schools in the Seattle area. She offers courses in tofu cooking, Thai cooking, vegetarian cooking, Northern Italian cooking, Brazilian cooking, and Indonesian cooking. She also does catering for special events and is a food consultant. Moreover, she is an avid organic gardener and an accomplished batik painter.

Ms. Ang lives in Seattle with her husband, Donald Richard Bissonnette, and two sons, Alex and André.

CHAPTER ONE

Condiments
&
Sauces

Condiments and Sauces

Cucumber Raita

2 tablespoons canola oil
1 tablespoon black
  mustard seeds
1/8 teaspoon asafoetida
1 tablespoon white lentils
  (Urad Dal), cooked
2 fresh red cayenne
  peppers, sliced (optional)
1/2 cup soft tofu, drained,
  mashed
1 cup plain yogurt
1 cucumber, peeled,
  shredded (carrots
  or radishes can also
  be used)

Heat the oil in a small pot and sauté the mustard seeds, asafoetida, lentils, and cayenne peppers for 1 minute. Pour the mixture into a large bowl. Add the tofu, yogurt and cucumber. Thoroughly mix the ingredients and refrigerate before serving. Serve with Samosa (see page 32) or Barbecued Tofu with Vegetables (see page 29).

Makes 2 cups.

Fresh Coriander Chutney

1 small yellow onion,
  chopped
3 cloves garlic, crushed
1 teaspoon salt
1 teaspoon sugar
 juice of 1 lemon
1 teaspoon cumin powder
1 tablespoon cumin seed
2 cups fresh coriander
  leaves, chopped
4 fresh, hot, green cayenne
  peppers, sliced
1/2 cup soft tofu, drained
1/2 cup roasted peanuts,
  crushed

In a blender, blend all the ingredients into a smooth sauce. Put into a tightly closed jar and refrigerate. Serve at room temperature. To be used with Samosa (see page 32) or Barbecued Tofu with Vegetables (see page 29).

Makes 2 cups.

CREAMY DILL DRESSING

1 cup soft tofu, drained
2 tablespoons fresh lemon
    juice
1 teaspoon salt
1/2 teaspoon ground white
    pepper
1 teaspoon Worcestershire
    sauce
2 teaspoons dill weed
1/2 cup plain yogurt

In a blender, blend the tofu, lemon juice, salt, white pepper, Worcestershire sauce, dill weed, and yogurt into a smooth sauce. Refrigerate before serving. To be used with vegetable salads.

Makes 2 cups.

HOLLANDAISE SAUCE

1 cup soft tofu, drained
1/2 teaspoon salt
1/2 cup canola oil
1 teaspoon sugar
juice of 1 lemon
1/2 teaspoon ground
    white pepper
1/4 teaspoon cayenne
    powder (optional)

In a blender, blend the tofu, salt, oil, sugar, lemon juice, pepper, and cayenne powder until smooth and creamy. Refrigerate before serving. To be used with vegetable salads.

Makes 1 1/2 cups.

Hot Sweet Sauce

1 cup light soy sauce
1/4 cup soft tofu, drained, mashed
1/2 cup brown sugar
2 fresh, hot, red cayenne peppers, sliced
3 cloves garlic, crushed
juice of 1 lime

Combine all the ingredients in a small pot and a simmer for 5 minutes. Cool and serve with Stuffed Nori with Crab (see page 92).

Makes 1 1/2 cups.

Italian Parsley Dressing

1 cup soft tofu, drained
1/2 cup plain yogurt
juice of 1 lemon
1/2 teaspoon sugar
2 teaspoons Worcestershire sauce
1/2 teaspoon ground white pepper
1 teaspoon salt
1/4 cup soy bean milk (see page 146) or regular milk
1/2 cup Italian parsley, finely chopped
2 tablespoons grated Parmesan cheese
1/4 cup green onion, finely chopped

In a blender, blend the tofu, yogurt, lemon juice, sugar, Worcestershire sauce, white pepper, salt, and milk into a smooth sauce. Pour the sauce into a small bowl and add the Italian parsley, Parmesan cheese, and green onion. Stir well and refrigerate before serving. To be used with vegetable salads.

Makes 2 cups.

Italian Tomato Sauce

3 tablespoons olive oil
1 large onion, finely
  chopped
4 cloves garlic, crushed
1/2 cup Italian parsley,
  chopped
2 carrots, peeled, chopped
1/2 cup dry white wine
2 fresh sage leaves,
  chopped
8 fresh basil leaves,
  chopped
1 teaspoon salt
1 cup soft tofu, drained
1/2 teaspoon ground black
  pepper
6 cups tomato sauce
1 can whole tomatoes
  (28 oz.)

Heat the oil in a large deep pot and sauté the onion and garlic until light golden brown. Add the parsley, carrots, wine, sage, basil, salt, tofu, pepper, tomato sauce and whole tomatoes. Cover and simmer for 40 minutes over low heat. Let cool. In a blender, blend the mixture into a smooth sauce. The Italian Tomato Sauce will keep 5 days when refrigerated and may also be frozen for longer storage. To be used with pasta dishes.

Makes 8 cups.

SAVORY GARLIC DRESSING

1 cup soft tofu, drained
4 cloves garlic, crushed
juice of 1 lemon
1 teaspoon salt
1/2 cup olive oil
3 tablespoons milk

In a blender, blend the tofu, garlic, lemon juice, and salt into a smooth paste. Pour the paste into a small bowl and add the olive oil and milk. Stir well and refrigerate before serving. To be used with vegetable salads.

Makes 1 cup.

SPICY LEMON DRESSING

1 cup soft tofu, drained
juice of 1 lemon
1 teaspoon curry powder
1/2 teaspoon cayenne
  powder
3 cloves garlic, crushed
1 teaspoon salt
1/2 cup canola oil
1/4 cup milk

In a blender, blend the tofu, lemon juice, curry powder, cayenne powder, garlic, and salt into a smooth paste. Pour the paste into a small bowl and add the canola oil and milk. Stir well and refrigerate before serving. To be used with vegetable salads.

Makes 2 cups.

Spicy Peanut Sauce

1/4 cup soft tofu, drained, mashed
4 cloves garlic, minced
4 fresh, hot, red cayenne peppers, sliced
juice of 1 lime
1/2 teaspoon salt
2 tablespoons brown sugar
1 tablespoon soy sauce
2 cups water
1 cup smooth or crunchy peanut butter

In a blender, blend the tofu, garlic, cayenne peppers, lime juice, salt, sugar and soy sauce until smooth. Pour the mixture into a large bowl and alternately add the water and peanut butter. Thoroughly mix with a wooden spoon. To be used with Tofu Satay (see page 34), Barbecued Tofu with Vegetables (see page 29) or vegetable salads.

Makes 3 cups.

Tarragon Tofu Dressing

1 cup olive oil
3 tablespoons Dijon mustard
1 tablespoon fresh tarragon leaves
1/2 teaspoon salt
1/2 teaspoon ground black pepper
juice of 1 lemon
3 cloves garlic, crushed
1 cup soft tofu, drained

In a blender, blend the oil, mustard, tarragon leaves, salt, pepper, lemon juice, garlic and tofu until smooth and creamy. Refrigerate before serving. To be used with vegetable salads.

Makes 2 cups.

TARTAR SAUCE

1 cup soft tofu, drained
1/2 cup fresh lemon juice
1/2 cup canola oil
2 tablespoons sugar
1 teaspoon mustard
1 teaspoon salt
1 small onion, finely
   chopped
1/2 cup sweet pickle relish

In a blender, blend the tofu, lemon juice, oil, sugar, mustard, and salt until smooth and creamy. Pour the tofu mixture in a bowl and add the onion and pickle relish. Mix well and refrigerate before serving. Serve with fried seafood.

Makes 2 1/2 cups.

TOFU LEMON MAYONNAISE

1 cup soft tofu, drained
juice of 1 lemon
1/2 teaspoon salt
1/2 teaspoon mustard
1 teaspoon honey
1/4 cup canola oil

In a blender, blend the tofu, lemon juice, salt, mustard, honey and oil until smooth and creamy. Refrigerate before serving. Serve with Tofuburgers with Herbs (see page 81).

Makes 1 1/2 cups.

Tofu Tomato Salsa

1 cucumber, peeled, cubed
1 pkg. extra firm tofu
  (12.4 oz.), drained, cubed
2 large ripe avocados,
  peeled, seeded, cubed
2 large tomatoes, chopped
1 small yellow onion,
  chopped
1 cup fresh coriander leaves,
  chopped
1 teaspoon salt
2 fresh, hot, green cayenne
  peppers, chopped
  (optional)
1/2 cup olive oil
juice of 2 limes

In a large salad bowl, thoroughly mix the cucumber, tofu, avocados, tomatoes, onion, coriander leaves, salt, cayenne peppers, olive oil, and lime juice. Chill for 30 minutes or overnight before serving. Serve with grilled vegetables or meats.

Makes 4 cups.

White Clam Sauce

3 tablespoons butter
2 cloves garlic, crushed
2 tablespoons flour
1/2 cup soft tofu, mashed
2 tablespoons dry white
  wine
3 tablespoons Italian parsley,
  finely chopped
1/2 teaspoon dried basil
1/2 teaspoon salt
3 cans minced clams
  (7 oz. each)

Melt the butter in a small pan and sauté the garlic until light golden brown. Add the flour and stir for a few seconds. Add the tofu, wine, parsley, basil, salt, and clams. Cover and simmer for 5 minutes, stirring occasionally. Serve with Spinach Tofu Noodles (see page 126).

Serves 4.

CHAPTER TWO

APPETIZERS

&

SNACKS

Appetizers and Snacks

ALMOND DIP

1 cup soft tofu, drained
3 tablespoons fresh
  lemon juice
2 tablespoons olive oil
1/2 teaspoon salt
1/2 cup roasted, slivered
  almonds

In a blender, blend the tofu, lemon juice, oil, and salt until smooth and creamy. Fold in the roasted slivered almonds. Chill before serving. Serve with fresh vegetables, toasted bread, or chips.

Makes 1 1/2 cups.

CRAB DIP

1 cup soft tofu, drained,
  mashed
1/2 cup yogurt
2 tablespoons fresh
  lemon juice
1/2 teaspoon salt
1/2 teaspoon cayenne
  powder
2 cloves garlic, minced
1 small yellow onion, finely
  chopped
1 cup canned crab meat
1/4 cup fresh coriander,
  chopped

In a large bowl, thoroughly mix the tofu, yogurt, lemon juice, salt, cayenne powder, garlic, onion, and crab meat. Garnish with the coriander leaves. Refrigerate before serving. Serve with fresh vegetables, toasted bread, or chips.

Makes 2 1/2 cups.

CRAB SPREAD

1 cup soft tofu, drained,
   mashed
1 cup cream cheese
1 small yellow onion, finely
   chopped
1 cup canned crab meat
1/2 teaspoon salt
1/2 teaspoon dry mustard
1 tablespoon fresh lemon
   juice
2 tablespoons green onion,
   chopped
1 teaspoon paprika

In a large bowl, mix the tofu and cream cheese with a wooden spoon until very smooth. Add the onion, crab meat, salt, mustard, lemon juice, and green onion. Stir well and sprinkle with the paprika. Serve with fresh vegetables, toasted bread, or chips.

Makes 3 cups.

GUACAMOLE

3 soft avocados, peeled,
   seeded, sliced
1/2 cup soft tofu, drained
2 tablespoons sour cream
juice of 1 lemon
1 teaspoon salt
1/2 teaspoon cayenne
   powder
1 teaspoon cumin powder
1 small yellow onion,
   chopped
1 small red tomato, chopped
1/4 cup fresh coriander
   leaves, chopped
2 tablespoons olive oil

In a large bowl, mash the avocados and tofu until they form a smooth paste. Add the sour cream, lemon juice, salt, cayenne powder, cumin, and onion. Mix well and garnish with the chopped tomato, coriander leaves and olive oil. Refrigerate before serving. Serve with corn chips or unflavored tortilla chips.

Makes 2 cups.

HOT CURRY DIP

1 cup soft tofu, drained,
   mashed
3 cloves garlic, crushed
1 teaspoon cayenne powder
2 tablespoons curry powder
juice of 1 lemon
1/2 teaspoon salt

In a blender, blend the tofu, garlic, cayenne powder, curry powder, lemon juice, and salt until smooth and creamy. Serve with fresh vegetables or crackers.

Makes 1 cup.

MUSHROOM DIP

1 tablespoon butter or
   margarine
2 cups fresh mushrooms,
   washed, drained, sliced
1 teaspoon salt
2 tablespoons green onion,
   chopped
1 cup soft tofu, drained,
   mashed
1/2 cup sour cream
1/2 teaspoon paprika

Melt the butter in a large frying pan and sauté the mushrooms for 2 minutes. In a large bowl, thoroughly mix the mushrooms, salt, green onion, tofu, and sour cream. Sprinkle with the paprika. Serve with fresh vegetables or crackers.

Makes 2 cups.

SALMON SPREAD

1 cup soft tofu, drained, mashed
1 cup cream cheese
1 small yellow onion, finely chopped
1 cup canned salmon meat
1 tablespoon fresh lemon juice
1 teaspoon dry mustard
2 tablespoons capers, minced
1/2 teaspoon ground white pepper
2 tablespoons green onion, chopped
1 teaspoon paprika

In a large bowl, mix the tofu and cream cheese with a wooden spoon until very smooth. Add the onion, salmon, lemon juice, mustard, capers, pepper, and green onion. Stir well and sprinkle with the paprika. Serve with fresh vegetables or toasted bread.

Makes 3 cups.

SHRIMP DIP

1 cup soft tofu, drained, mashed
1/2 cup yogurt
2 tablespoons fresh lemon juice
1 teaspoon salt
1 cup cooked baby shrimp
1 teaspoon paprika
1 tablespoon green onion, finely chopped
1 small yellow onion, finely chopped
1 teaspoon dill weed

In a large bowl, thoroughly mix the tofu, yogurt, lemon juice, salt, baby shrimp, paprika, green onion, onion, and dill weed. Refrigerate overnight before serving. Serve with fresh vegetables or chips.

Makes 2 1/2 cups.

SPINACH DIP

1 lb. spinach, cleaned,
washed
1 cup soft tofu, drained,
mashed
1/4 cup Italian parsley,
finely chopped
1/2 cup sour cream
2 tablespoons fresh
lemon juice
1 teaspoon salt
1 teaspoon dill weed
2 tablespoons olive oil
1 teaspoon paprika

Blanch the spinach and drain well, squeezing out the excess water. Chop the spinach very fine. In a large bowl, mix the spinach, tofu, parsley, sour cream, lemon juice, salt, dill weed, and olive oil. Sprinkle with the paprika. Refrigerate before serving. Serve with fresh vegetables or chips.

Makes 3 cups.

TAHINI TOFU DIP

1 cup soft tofu, drained
1/4 cup tahini (sesame paste)
2 tablespoons soy bean
paste (Brown Rice Miso)
1/4 cup Italian parsley,
finely chopped
juice of 1 lemon
1 tablespoon pine nuts

In a blender, blend the tofu, tahini, soy bean paste, Italian parsley, and lemon juice into a smooth paste. Garnish with the pine nuts. Serve with fresh vegetables or chips.

Makes 1 1/2 cups.

Tofu Humus

1/2 cup firm tofu, drained
4 cloves garlic, crushed
juice of 1 lemon
1/3 cup tahini (sesame
  paste)
2 cups canned garbanzo
  beans, drained
1/2 teaspoon salt
1/4 cup Italian parsley,
  finely chopped
2 tablespoons olive oil
1/2 teaspoon paprika

In a blender, blend the tofu, garlic, lemon juice, tahini, garbanzo beans, salt, and Italian parsley until very smooth. Pour the tofu humus into a bowl and sprinkle with the olive oil and paprika. Serve with Pita bread.

Serves 4-6.

Tofu Liver Spread

2 tablespoons canola oil
1 small yellow onion,
  chopped
3 cloves garlic, crushed
1 lb. beef liver, washed
1 teaspoon salt
1 teaspoon ground nutmeg
1/2 cup soft tofu, drained
1 teaspoon paprika

Heat the oil in a small pot and sauté the onion and garlic until light golden brown. Add the liver, salt, and nutmeg and sauté for 5 minutes or until the liver is cooked. Add the tofu and simmer for about 2 minutes, stirring occasionally. Let cool. Pour the liver mixture into a blender and blend until smooth. Sprinkle with the paprika before serving. Serve with fresh vegetables, toasted bread or crackers.

Makes 2 cups.

BARBECUED TOFU WITH VEGETABLES

2 tablespoons olive oil
1 small green zucchini,
  cubed
1 pkg. extra firm tofu
  (12.4 oz.), drained, cubed
1 large red bell pepper,
  seeded, cubed
1 large green bell pepper,
  seeded, cubed
1 large yellow onion, cubed
2 cups fresh mushrooms,
  washed, drained
1 teaspoon ground white
  pepper
1 teaspoon salt
juice of 1 lemon
6 cloves garlic, crushed
1 cup Italian parsley,
  finely chopped
6" bamboo skewers, soaked
  in water for 15 minutes,
  drained

Place the oil, zucchini, tofu, red bell pepper, green bell pepper, onion, and mushrooms in a large bowl. Set aside. In a small bowl, thoroughly mix the pepper, salt, lemon juice, garlic, and Italian parsley. Pour this mixture over the cubed tofu and vegetables. Marinate for at least 1 hour or overnight in a refrigerator. Alternate vegetables and tofu cubes on bamboo skewers. Broil over a hot charcoal fire until cooked thoroughout, or broil in the oven for 3 minutes on each side. Serve with Tofu Tomato Salsa (see page 20).

Serves 4-6.

CALZONE

Dough

1 tablespoon yeast
1 cup warm water
2 cups white flour
1 cup whole wheat flour
2 tablespoons olive oil
1/2 teaspoon salt
1/2 teaspoon sugar

Filling

1/2 cup soft tofu, drained, mashed
4 cloves garlic, crushed
1 red bell pepper, seeded, chopped
1/2 cup ricotta cheese
1/2 cup grated mozzarella cheese
1/2 cup grated provolone cheese
1/2 teaspoon dried oregano
4 sweet basil leaves, chopped
1 yolk, beaten
1 tablespoon olive oil

In a small bowl, dissolve the yeast in the warm water. Combine the white and whole wheat flour in a large bowl and make a well in the middle. Pour the yeast mixture, oil, salt, and sugar into the well. Stir to form a smooth dough. Turn out on a smooth floured surface and knead for 3 minutes, or until the dough is smooth. Place the dough in an oiled bowl and let sit for 40 minutes or until it doubles in size. In a large bowl, mix the tofu, garlic, bell pepper, ricotta, mozzarella, provolone, oregano, and basil. Set aside. Divide the dough into 4 pieces and shape each into a ball. Roll out into 7-inch circles on a lightly floured surface. Spread 1/2 cup of the filling over 1/2 of each circle, leaving 1/2 inch of the outside bare. Fold the bare side over the filling. Crimp the edges together with a fork. Place the filled dough on oiled cookie sheets and slash the tops of each calzone twice, 2 inches apart. Brush the top of each calzone with the egg yolk and olive oil. Bake in a 425 degree oven for 25 minutes or until the top is golden brown.

Makes 4.

EMPANADAS

3 cups flour, sifted
1/2 teaspoon salt
2/3 cup butter or margarine
3 tablespoons cold water
4 egg yolks
2 tablespoons canola oil
1 small yellow onion, finely
  chopped
3 cloves garlic, minced
1 lb. extra lean ground beef
2 tablespoons raisins
1/2 cup stuffed green olives,
  sliced
1 teaspoon salt
1/2 teaspoon cayenne
  powder
1 tablespoon cumin powder
1 teaspoon paprika
1/2 cup firm tofu, drained,
  mashed
2 fresh, red cayenne
  peppers, chopped
  (optional)
2 tablespoons flour
2 hard boiled eggs, cut into
  4 wedges each

Make the dough in a large bowl by thoroughly mixing the 3 cups of flour, salt, butter, cold water and 2 of the egg yolks. Set aside. Heat the oil in a large frying pan and sauté the onion and garlic until light golden brown. Add the ground beef, raisins, green olives, salt, cayenne powder, cumin, and paprika. Sauté for 3 minutes and add the tofu, cayenne peppers and 2 tablespoons of flour. Sauté for 2 minutes, stirring frequently. Let cool. Roll out the dough into circles 4 inches in diameter and 1/8" thick. Put 1 tablespoon of the filling halfway from the edge. Place 1 slice of hard boiled egg on top of the filling. Fold the bare side over the filling. Crimp the edges together with a fork. Brush each one with the remaining 2 beaten egg yolks. Bake in a 375 degree oven for 20 minutes or until the top of the dough is light golden brown.

Makes 8.

SAMOSA

Filling
2 tablespoons butter
1 teaspoon black mustard
  seeds
1 teaspoon fresh ground
  ginger
1 small yellow onion, chopped
1 cup firm tofu, drained, cubed
1 cup frozen green peas
1 large potato, cooked, cubed
juice of 1 lemon
1 teapoon ground cumin
1 tablespoon garam masala
1 tablespoon curry powder
1/2 teaspoon salt
1/4 cup fresh coriander leaves,
  finely chopped
2 cups canola oil for
  deep-frying

Dough
2 cups flour
1/4 teaspoon salt
1/4 cup butter, melted
1/3 cup plain yogurt
2 tablespoons cold water

Melt the butter in a large pot and sauté the mustard seeds, ginger, and onion for 2 minutes or until light golden brown. Add the tofu, green peas, potato, lemon juice, cumin, masala, curry powder, salt and fresh coriander leaves. Sauté for 3 minutes. Let cool before stuffing. In a large bowl, make the pastry by mixing all the dough ingredients and kneading it until smooth and elastic, about 5-10 minutes. Roll out to 1/8-inch thin on a floured board. Cut into 4-inch circles. Place 2 tablespoons of filling in the center of each circle, leaving 1/2-inch edges free. Fold over and seal by crimping with the tines of a fork. Repeat the same procedure until all the dough is used. Deep-fry in hot oil until golden brown or bake in a 350 degree oven for 20 minutes or until the top is golden brown. Remove and drain on paper towels. Serve with Fresh Coriander Chutney (see page 13).

Makes 4-6.

STUFFED MUSHROOMS

2 tablespoons olive oil
20 large fresh mushrooms, washed, drained, stems removed and reserved
1 cup soft tofu, drained, mashed
3 cloves garlic, crushed
1/4 cup Italian parsley, chopped
1/2 teaspoon salt
1/2 teaspoon ground black pepper
1/2 teaspoon nutmeg
2 tablespoons green onion, chopped
1/4 cup ricotta cheese
1/2 cup grated mozzarella cheese
1/4 cup Parmesan cheese
1/4 cup bread crumbs
1 teaspoon paprika

Heat the oil in a large frying pan and sauté the mushroom caps for 1 minute or until light golden brown on both sides. Remove and drain on paper towels. Set aside. Chop the stems of the mushrooms and place them in a large bowl. Mix them with the tofu, garlic, parsley, salt, pepper, nutmeg, green onion, ricotta and mozzarella cheese. Fill each mushroom cap with the tofu mixture and place them on an oiled, 9x13 inch baking pan. Sprinkle with the Parmesan cheese, bread crumbs, and paprika. Bake in a 375 degree oven for 10 minutes or until the top is golden brown.

Serves 6-8.

Tofu Satay

1 stalk fresh lemon grass, finely chopped
1 teaspoon brown sugar
2 tablespoons canola oil
2 pkgs. extra firm tofu (12.4 oz. each), drained, cut into 1-inch cubes
1 large yellow onion, cubed
1 cup mushrooms, washed, drained
1 large red bell pepper, seeded, cubed
6 cloves garlic, crushed
1 tablespoon ground coriander
1 tablespoon ground cumin
1 tablespoon ground turmeric
1 teaspoon ground white pepper
1 teaspoon salt
juice of 1 lime
1/2 cup fresh coriander leaves, finely chopped
1/2 cup coconut milk
6" bamboo skewers, soaked in water for 15 minutes, drained

In a large bowl, thoroughly mix the lemon grass, sugar, oil, tofu, onion, mushrooms, red bell pepper, garlic, coriander, cumin, turmeric, pepper, salt, lime juice, coriander leaves and coconut milk. Marinate this mixture for at least 1 hour or overnight in a refrigerator. Alternate tofu, onion cubes, mushrooms, and red bell pepper on bamboo skewers. Broil over a hot charcoal fire until cooked throughout, or broil in the oven for 2 minutes on each side. Serve with Spicy Peanut Sauce (see page 18).

Serves 4-6.

TOFU SPANAKOPITA

3 tablespoons olive oil
1 small yellow onion, chopped
4 cloves garlic, crushed
4 pkgs. chopped frozen spinach (10 oz. each), thawed, squeezed dry
1/2 cup Italian parsley, chopped
1/4 cup green onion, chopped
1 cup firm tofu, drained, mashed
1 cup feta cheese, finely crumbled
3 eggs, beaten
1 teaspoon ground black pepper
2 tablespoons dill weed
1 pkg. filo leaves (1 lb.)
1 cup butter, melted

Heat the oil in a small pot and sauté the onion and garlic until light golden brown. Add the spinach, parsley, green onion, tofu and feta cheese. Stir-fry for 2 minutes. Transfer the spinach mixture to a deep bowl and add the eggs, pepper, and dill weed. Mix well and cool to room temperature. Divide the package of filo leaves in two. One half is for the bottom layer; the other half is for the top layer. Put a damp tea towel on top of each pile. If the leaves fall apart, do not worry, just lay the broken pieces on top of each other. Place one or two leaves in the bottom of a buttered 9x13 baking pan and lightly butter them with a pastry brush. Continue to do this until all the leaves are used. Next, place the spinach/tofu filling in the baking pan. Take the remaining half of the filo leaves and spread them on top of the spinach/tofu filling in the same way as in the bottom of the pan. Bake in a 350 degree oven for 40 minutes or until the top is golden brown.

Serves 6-8.

TOFU WITH JAMAICAN JERK SAUCE

2 tablespoons canola oil
2 pkgs. extra firm tofu
(12.4 oz. each), drained,
cut into 1-inch cubes
1 large yellow onion, cubed
1 large red bell pepper,
cubed
2 cups fresh mushrooms,
washed, drained
1 large green zucchini,
seeded, cubed
1/2 teaspoon honey
1 teaspoon brown sugar
2 green jalapeno peppers
5 cloves garlic, crushed
1 tablespoon fresh ginger,
chopped
1/4 cup Italian parsley
6 fresh basil leaves
1 teaspoon ground
cinnamon
1/2 teaspoon allspice
1 teaspoon salt
1 teaspoon ground black
pepper
3 tablespoons Dijon mustard
2 tablespoons fresh lime
juice
2 tablespoons red wine
vinegar
6" bamboo skewers, soaked
in water for 15 minutes,
drained

Place the oil, tofu, onion, bell pepper, mushrooms, and zucchini in a large bowl. Set aside. In a blender, blend the honey, sugar, jalapenos, garlic, ginger, parsley, basil leaves, cinnamon, allspice, salt, pepper, mustard, lime juice, and vinegar into a smooth paste. Pour this mixture over the cubed tofu and vegetables. Marinate for at least 1 hour or overnight in a refrigerator. Alternate vegetables and tofu cubes on the bamboo skewers. Broil over a hot charcoal fire until cooked thoroughout, or broil in the oven for 3 minutes on each side. The same Jamaican jerk sauce can be used for beef, pork or chicken barbecue.

Serves 4-6.

CHAPTER THREE

SOUPS

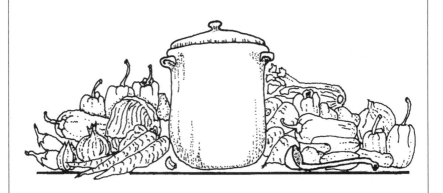

CHAPTER THREE

Soups

BORSCHT

2 tablespoons butter or
margarine
1 small red onion, chopped
2 large potatoes, peeled,
cubed
4 beets, peeled, cubed
1 large carrot, peeled, cubed
1 teaspoon caraway seeds
6 cups water
1/4 cup fresh lemon juice
1 teaspoon salt
1/2 teaspoon ground black
pepper
1 teaspoon dill weed
1 tablespoon honey
1 pkg. extra firm tofu
(12.4 oz.), drained, cubed
1 cup sour cream
1/4 cup green onion,
chopped

Melt the butter in a large pot and sauté the onion until light golden brown. Add the potatoes, beets, carrot, caraway seeds, water, lemon juice, salt, pepper, dill weed, and honey. Bring to a boil and reduce the heat to low. Cover and simmer for 30 minutes or until the vegetables are soft. Add the tofu and simmer for 3 minutes. Add 1 tablespoon of sour cream to each bowl of Borscht just before serving. Garnish with the green onion. Serve either hot or at room temperature.

Serves 6-8.

CORN AND SHRIMP SOUP

2 tablespoons canola oil
1 yellow onion, finely
  chopped
3 cloves garlic, crushed
8 cups water
2 cans creamed corn
  (17 oz. each)
2 cups whole frozen corn
1 large red bell pepper,
  seeded, cubed
2 stalks celery, chopped
1 small potato, peeled,
  cubed
1 cup firm tofu, drained,
  cubed
1 teaspoon salt
1/2 teaspoon ground black
  pepper
2 bay leaves
1 teaspoon dry thyme
1 cup baby shrimp, cooked
2 tablespoons cornstarch,
  dissolved in a 1/4 cup of
  cold water
2 green onions, chopped
1/4 cup fresh coriander
  leaves, chopped

Heat the oil in a large pot and sauté the onion and garlic until light golden brown. Add the water, cream of corn, whole corn, bell pepper, celery, potato, tofu, salt, pepper, bay leaves, and thyme. Bring the mixture to a boil, then reduce the temperature to low. Simmer for 20 minutes or until the vegetables are soft. Add the shrimp and cornstarch mixture. Stir well and simmer for 3 minutes. Garnish with the green onions and coriander leaves.

Serves 6-8.

CREAMY EGGPLANT SOUP

2 tablespoons butter or
  margarine
1 small yellow onion,
  chopped
2 cloves garlic, crushed
1 small eggplant, cubed
2 large potatoes, peeled,
  cubed
3 stalks celery, chopped
1 teaspoon salt
1 teaspoon dried thyme
5 cups chicken stock or
  vegetable stock
1/2 teaspoon ground white
  pepper
1 pkg. firm tofu (16 oz.),
  drained, cubed
1 cup soy bean milk (see
  page 146) or regular milk
1/2 teaspoon brown sugar
3 tablespoons cornstarch
1 cup soft tofu, drained
1/4 cup green onion,
  chopped

Heat the butter in a large pot and sauté the onion and garlic until light golden brown. Add the eggplant, potatoes, celery, salt, and thyme and sauté for 2 more minutes, stirring frequently. Add the chicken stock, pepper and tofu. Simmer for 10 minutes or until the vegetables are soft. Combine the soy milk, sugar, cornstarch, and soft tofu in a blender and blend until very smooth. Stir this mixture into the soup and continue stirring until the soup thickens. Simmer for 1 more minute. Garnish with the green onion.

Serves 4-6.

CREAMY LEEK SOUP

2 tablespoons butter or
  margarine
1 small yellow onion,
  chopped
3 cloves garlic, crushed
4 leeks, chopped
1 cup dry white wine
2 large potatoes, peeled,
  cubed
4 cups water
2 cups soft tofu, drained,
  mashed
1/2 teaspoon ground white
  pepper
1 teaspoon salt
1/4 cup Italian parsley,
  chopped
2 cups soy bean milk (see
  page 146) or regular milk
1/4 cup green onion,
  chopped
1/4 cup fresh coriander
  leaves, chopped

Melt the butter in a large deep pot and sauté the onion and garlic until light golden brown. Add the leeks and sauté for 2 more minutes. Add the wine, potatoes, water, tofu, pepper, salt, and Italian parsley. Simmer for 40 minutes or until the vegetables are soft. Cool. Pour the mixture in a blender and blend until smooth and creamy. Return to the pot and add the soy milk. Simmer over low heat for 5 minutes. Garnish with the green onion and coriander leaves.

Serves 6-8.

CREAMY MUSHROOM SOUP

2 tablespoons butter or
  margarine
1 small yellow onion,
  chopped
2 cloves garlic, chopped
2 cups fresh mushrooms,
  washed, sliced
2 large potatoes, peeled,
  cubed
2 stalks celery, chopped
1 large carrot, peeled,
  chopped
1 teaspoon salt
1 teaspoon dried thyme
5 cups chicken or vegetable
  stock
1/2 teaspoon ground white
  pepper
1 pkg. firm tofu (16 oz.),
  drained, cubed
1 cup soy bean milk (see
  page 146) or regular milk
1/2 teaspoon brown sugar
3 tablespoons cornstarch
1 cup soft tofu, drained
1/4 cup fresh coriander
  leaves, chopped
4 green onions, chopped

Melt the butter in a large pot and sauté the onion and garlic until light golden brown. Add the mushrooms, potatoes, celery, carrot, salt, and thyme and sauté for 3 minutes, stirring frequently. Add the chicken stock, pepper and tofu. Simmer for 10 minutes or until the vegetables are soft. Combine the soy milk, sugar, cornstarch, and tofu in the blender and blend until very smooth. Stir this mixture into the soup and continue stirring until the soup thickens. Simmer for 2 more minutes. Garnish with the coriander leaves and green onions.

Serves 4-6.

HEARTY VEGETABLE SOUP

2 tablespoons olive oil
1 large yellow onion,
   chopped
3 cloves garlic, chopped
1/2 cup dry white wine
4 cups canned whole
   tomatoes
4 cups water
1 red bell pepper, seeded,
   chopped
4 stalks celery, chopped
2 large carrots, chopped
1 leek, chopped
2 large potatoes, chopped
1 large zucchini, chopped
4 fresh basil leaves,
   chopped
1 teaspoon fresh oregano
1 teaspoon fresh thyme
1 teaspoon salt
1/2 teaspoon ground black
   pepper
1 pkg. extra firm tofu
   (12.4 oz.), drained, cubed
1/4 cup grated Parmesan
   cheese (optional)
1/4 cup Italian parsley,
   chopped

Heat the oil in a large deep pot and sauté the onion and garlic until light golden brown. Add the wine, tomatoes and water. Bring to a boil and add the red bell pepper, celery, carrots, leek, potatoes, zucchini, basil leaves, oregano, thyme, salt, and pepper. Simmer for 20 minutes or until the vegetables are soft. Add the tofu and simmer for 5 more minutes. Garnish with the Parmesan cheese and Italian parsley.

Serves 6-8.

LEMON SOUP

4 cups chicken broth
1 pkg. firm tofu (16 oz.),
  drained, cubed
2 cups milk
1 cup cooked rice
1/4 cup fresh lemon juice
  dissolved with 2
  tablespoons cornstarch
1/2 teaspoon salt
1/2 teaspoon ground white
  pepper
1/4 cup Italian parsley,
  chopped
1/4 cup grated Parmesan
  cheese (optional)
1/4 cup green onion,
  chopped

In an uncovered, large deep pot, bring the chicken broth, tofu, and milk to a boil. Add the rice and simmer for 15 minutes. Slowly add the lemon juice mixture, stirring constantly for 1 minute. Add the salt, pepper, and Italian parsley. Stir and simmer for a few seconds. Garnish with the Parmesan cheese and green onion.

Serves 4-6.

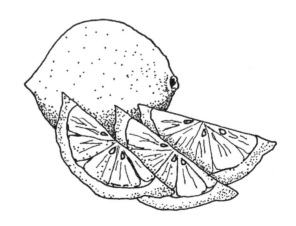

MINESTRONE SOUP

1/4 cup olive oil
1 pkg. firm tofu (16 oz.),
   frozen then thawed,
   drained, cut into 1-inch
   cubes
2 tablespoons butter or
   margarine
1 small yellow onion, finely
   chopped
3 cloves garlic, crushed
2 stalks celery, chopped
2 carrots, peeled, cubed
1 large zucchini, cubed
1 red bell pepper, seeded,
   cubed
1 can whole tomatoes
   (28 oz.), chopped
3 cups tomato juice
3 cups water
1/4 cup fresh Italian parsley,
   chopped
1 teaspoon fresh oregano
6 fresh basil leaves,
   chopped
1/2 teaspoon ground black
   pepper
1 teaspoon salt
1/2 cup broken spaghetti,
   uncooked
1 can kidney beans (15 oz.)
1/2 cup grated Parmesan
   cheese

Heat the oil in a large frying pan and fry the tofu until crispy on both sides. Remove and drain on paper towels. Set aside. Melt the butter in a large deep pot and sauté the onion and garlic until light golden brown. Add the celery, carrots, zucchini, and bell pepper. Sauté for 3 more minutes. Add the chopped whole tomatoes, tomato juice, water, Italian parsley, oregano, basil leaves, pepper, salt, spaghetti, and kidney beans. Simmer for 20 minutes or until the vegetables are cooked. Garnish with the Parmesan cheese.

Serves 6-8.

Miso Soup with Vegetables

4 cups water
1 large carrot, thinly sliced
8 fresh mushrooms, washed,
  drained, sliced
2 cloves garlic, crushed
1 pkg. firm tofu (16 oz.),
  drained, cubed
3 tablespoons soy bean
  paste   (Brown Rice Miso),
  dissolved in 1/4 cup warm
  water
4 green onions, chopped
1/4 cup fresh coriander
  leaves, chopped

Bring the water to a boil in a large pot and add the carrot, mushrooms, and garlic. Let simmer for 10 minutes. Add the cubed tofu and miso. Simmer for 2 more minutes. Garnish with the green onions and coriander leaves.

Serves 4-6.

Miso Spinach Soup

4 cups water
1 pkg. firm tofu (16 oz.),
  drained, cubed
3 tablespoons soy bean
  paste (Brown Rice Miso)
1 lb. fresh spinach, cleaned
1 tablespoon sesame oil

Bring the water to a boil in a large pot. Reduce the heat to low and add the tofu and miso and simmer for 3 minutes. Stir in the spinach and sesame oil and simmer for 1 more minute. (Do not overcook the spinach.) Serve hot.

Serves 4-6.

ONION SOUP

2 tablespoons butter or
  margarine
2 large yellow onions,
  chopped
3 cloves garlic, crushed
2 tablespoons flour
6 cups water or vegetable
  stock
1/2 cup dry white wine
1/2 teaspoon ground white
  pepper
1 teaspoon salt
1 cup frozen tofu, thawed,
  drained, cut into 1/2-inch
  cubes
1/2 cup grated Parmesan
  cheese
1 tablespoon paprika

Melt the butter in a large pot and sauté the onions and garlic until light golden brown. Add the flour and sauté for 1 minute. Add the water, wine, pepper, and salt. Simmer for 20 minutes. Fill 6 individual oven-proof bowls with soup. On top of the soup in each bowl, put 2 tablespoons of tofu cubes and sprinkle with the Parmesan cheese and paprika. Bake for about 5 minutes in a preheated oven at 400 degrees or until the top is golden brown.

Serves 6.

Seaweed Soup

8 cups chicken stock
1 pkg. firm tofu (16 oz.),
  drained, cubed
4 sheets of nori (8x8)
  (seaweed sheets), cut
  into 1-inch squares
1 teaspoon salt
2 egg whites, beaten
1 tablespoon sesame oil
4 green onions, chopped
1/4 cup fresh coriander
  leaves, chopped

In a large deep pot, bring the chicken stock to a boil. Add the tofu, seaweed, and salt, then bring it back to a boil for 2 minutes. Pour the beaten egg whites slowly into the soup and simmer for 1 minute. Sprinkle with the sesame oil and garnish with the green onions and coriander leaves.

Serves 4-6.

Seaweed with Tofu Soup

2 tablespoons sesame oil
1 strip kombu seaweed, 8
  inches long, soaked in
  water for 10 minutes,
  washed, drained, cubed
3 cloves garlic, crushed
1 small yellow onion,
  chopped
1 large tomato, cubed
1 teaspoon salt
6 cups water
1 pkg. firm tofu (16 oz.),
  drained, cubed
4 green onions, chopped

Heat the oil in a large deep pot and sauté the seaweed, garlic, and onion until light brown. Add the tomato and salt and sauté for 2 minutes. Add the water and bring it to a boil. Reduce the heat to low and simmer for 10 minutes. Add the tofu and simmer for 3 more minutes. Garnish with the green onions.

Serves 4-6.

SPICY PRAWN SOUP

6 cups water
1 lb. medium-sized prawns,
  shelled, deveined (see
  diagram, page 149)
2 stalks fresh lemon grass,
  sliced
1 can straw mushrooms
  (8 oz.), drained
1 can baby corn (15 oz.),
  drained
1 pkg. firm tofu (16 oz.),
  drained, cubed
4 kaffir lime leaves
1/4 cup fish sauce (Nam Pla)
juice of 1 lime
2 fresh red cayenne peppers,
  sliced
4 green onions, chopped
1/4 cup fresh coriander
  leaves, chopped

Bring the water to a boil in a large pot. Add the prawns, lemon grass, mushrooms, baby corn, tofu, lime leaves, fish sauce, lime juice and cayenne peppers. Reduce the heat to low and cook for 5 minutes. Garnish with the green onions and coriander leaves.

Serves 4-6.

Spicy Sweet and Sour Soup

8 cups vegetable or chicken
stock
1 large carrot, peeled, cut
into julienne strips
1 cup bamboo shoots, cut
into julienne strips
1 cup firm tofu, cut into
julienne strips
1 teaspoon cayenne powder
juice of 1 lime
1/2 teaspoon salt
2 tablespoons soy sauce
1 tablespoon sugar
6 dried black Chinese
mushrooms, soaked in 1/4
cup of warm water for 10
minutes (reserve the
water), cut into julienne
strips (Note: Remove
the hard ends from the
stems.)
1/4 cup cornstarch,
dissolved in 1/4 cup of
cold water
2 eggs, beaten
1 tablespoon sesame oil
4 green onions, chopped
1/4 cup fresh coriander
leaves, chopped

Bring the vegetable stock to a boil in a large deep pot. Add the carrot, bamboo shoots, tofu, cayenne powder, lime juice, salt, soy sauce, sugar, black Chinese mushrooms, and reserved mushroom soaking water. Simmer for 10 minutes. Stir the cornstarch mixture into the soup until it thickens slightly. Stir well and gradually add in the beaten eggs. Sprinkle with the sesame oil and garnish with the green onions and coriander leaves.

Serves 6-8.

51

THAI CHICKEN SOUP WITH TOFU

6 cups water
1/2 lb. boneless chicken
  breast, thinly sliced
2 tablespoons cornstarch
1 pkg. firm tofu (16 oz.),
  drained, cubed
1 pkg. cellophane noodles
  (3 1/2 oz.), soaked in warm
  water for 5 minutes,
  drained
1 can straw mushrooms
  (8 oz.), drained
1 can baby corn (15 oz.),
  drained
1/4 cup shredded bamboo
  shoots, drained
1 teaspoon salt
1/2 teaspoon ground white
  pepper
4 green onions, cut
  into 2-inch lengths
1/4 cup fresh coriander
  leaves, chopped

Bring the water to a boil in a large pot. Coat the sliced chicken with the cornstarch and add it to the soup. Stir the soup and bring it back to a boil, then reduce it to a simmer for 5 minutes. Add the tofu, cellophane noodles, straw mushrooms, baby corn, bamboo shoots, salt, and pepper and simmer for 2 more minutes. Garnish with the green onions and coriander leaves.

Serves 4-6.

THAI PUMPKIN SOUP

2 tablespoons canola oil
1 small yellow onion,
  chopped
3 cloves garlic, crushed
4 cups water
1 stalk lemon grass, cut into
  2-inch lengths
1 one-inch piece dried Laos
  root (Kha)
2 cups fresh pumpkin, cubed
2 tablespoons fish sauce
  (Nam Pla)
1/2 teaspoon salt
1 cup canned coconut milk
1 pkg. firm tofu (16 oz.),
  frozen then thawed,
  drained, cubed
2 fresh red cayenne
  peppers, sliced
juice of 1 lime
1/4 cup fresh coriander
  leaves, chopped
1/4 cup green onion,
  chopped

Heat the oil in a large pot and sauté the onion and garlic until light golden brown. Add the water, lemon grass, Laos root, pumpkin, fish sauce, and salt. Simmer for 10 minutes or until the pumpkin is soft. Add the coconut milk, tofu, cayenne peppers and lime juice and simmer for 2 more minutes. Garnish with the coriander leaves and green onion.

Serves 4-6.

WONTON TOFU SOUP

1/4 lb. lean ground pork
1 egg, beaten
1/2 teaspoon salt
1/2 teaspoon ground white
   pepper
1 tablespoon sesame oil
1 cup firm tofu, drained,
   mashed
1 tablespoon cornstarch
1 pkg. wonton wrappers
2 quarts water
6 cups chicken broth
4 green onions, chopped

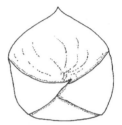

    In a small bowl, thoroughly mix the pork, egg, salt, pepper, sesame oil, tofu, and cornstarch. Place 1 teaspoon of the pork mixture in the center of each wonton wrapper. Wet the edges of the wrapper and fold it up, corner to corner, pinching together the 3 corners so that the filled wonton folds up into a triangle. Next, wet one of the bottom corners of the triangle and fold it over to join with the opposite corner with both sides overlapping and then pinching them together (see diagram, page 148). (Another method of filling the wonton wrappers is to wet the four corners and bunch them together to form a flower.) In a medium-sized pot, bring the chicken broth to a boil and set it aside. In a deep pot, bring the water to a boil and drop the wontons into the boiling water, uncovered for 3 minutes. When the water boils again, add 1 cup of cold water, then bring it back to a boil for 1 minute. Remove the wontons with a slotted spoon. In small bowls, put 1 cup of the heated chicken broth and add 5 cooked wontons in each bowl. Garnish with the green onions.

Serves 4-6.

CHAPTER FOUR

SALADS

CHAPTER FOUR

Salads

ALMOND CHICKEN SALAD

2 cups cooked chicken
  breast, skinned, diced
1 pkg. extra firm tofu
  (12.4 oz.), drained, cubed
1 cup celery, diced
1 large carrot, peeled,
  shredded
4 green onions, chopped
1 small yellow onion, finely
  chopped
2 tablespoons Italian parsley,
  chopped
1/2 cup slivered almonds,
  toasted
1 cup soft tofu, drained
1/2 cup olive oil
juice of 1 lemon
1 teaspoon honey
1 teaspoon salt
1/2 teaspoon ground black
  pepper
1 teaspoon paprika
1/4 cup fresh coriander
  leaves, chopped

In a large salad bowl, arrange the chicken, extra firm tofu, celery, carrot, green onions, yellow onion, Italian parsley, and toasted almonds in layers. In a blender, blend the soft tofu, olive oil, lemon juice, honey, salt, and pepper until very smooth and creamy. Pour the dressing over the salad and toss. Sprinkle with the paprika and garnish with the coriander leaves.

Serves 4-6.

Avocado Salad

1 head green leaf lettuce,
washed, drained
1 pkg. extra firm tofu
(12.4 oz.), drained, cut
into 1-inch cubes
2 ripe tomatoes, cubed
2 ripe avocados, seeded,
cubed
2 fresh green cayenne
peppers, chopped
1/2 cup red onion,
chopped
1/4 cup fresh coriander
leaves, chopped
3 cloves garlic, crushed
juice of 1 lime
1/2 cup olive oil
1 teaspoon salt
1/2 teaspoon ground black
pepper
1 teaspoon paprika

Place the lettuce leaves on a large serving platter and arrange the tofu, tomatoes, avocados, cayenne peppers, red onion, and fresh coriander leaves in layers. In a small bowl, thoroughly mix the garlic, lime juice, olive oil, salt and pepper. Pour the dressing over the salad. Sprinkle with the paprika. Chill before serving.

Serves 4-6.

Beet and Potato Salad

4 cups water
4 large beets, peeled, cubed
1 large potato, peeled, cubed
1 pkg. extra firm tofu
    (12.4 oz.), drained, cubed
1/2 cup celery, diced
1/2 cup yellow onion, finely
    chopped
1/2 teaspoon salt
2/3 cup Tofu Lemon
    Mayonnaise (see page 19)

Bring the water to a boil in a large pot. Add the beets and potato and cook for 15 minutes or until soft. Do not overcook. Drain the vegetables. In a large bowl, mix the cooked vegetables, tofu, celery, onion, salt, and mayonnaise. Refrigerate until ready to serve.

Serves 4-6.

Cole Slaw Salad

1 small green cabbage,
    thinly shredded
1 large carrot, peeled,
    shredded
4 green onions, chopped
1/4 cup Italian parsley,
    chopped
1 small yellow onion, finely
    chopped
1/2 cup raisins (optional)
1 cup soft tofu, drained,
    mashed
1/2 cup canola oil
juice of 1 lemon
1 tablespoon honey
1 teaspoon salt
1/2 teaspoon ground black
    pepper
1 teaspoon paprika

In a large salad bowl, arrange the green cabbage, carrot, green onions, Italian parsley, onion, and raisins in layers. In a blender, blend the tofu, oil, lemon, honey, salt, and pepper until very smooth and creamy. Pour over the salad and toss. Sprinkle with the paprika. Chill before serving.

Serves 4-6.

CURRIED CHICKEN SALAD

2 cups cooked chicken, skinned, diced
1 cup cooked string beans, diced
1 large boiled potato, diced
1 large boiled carrot, diced
1 small yellow onion, chopped
2 hard boiled eggs, diced
4 green onions, chopped
1 cup soft tofu, drained, mashed
1/2 cup Tofu Lemon Mayonnaise (see page 19)
1 teaspoon dry mustard
1 teaspoon salt
1/2 teaspoon ground white pepper
2 tablespoons curry powder
2 tablespoons fresh lemon juice
3 large tomatoes, thinly sliced
1/4 cup fresh coriander leaves, chopped

In a large bowl, thoroughly mix the cooked chicken, string beans, potato, carrot, onion, eggs, green onions, mashed tofu, mayonnaise, mustard, salt, pepper, curry powder, and lemon juice. Arrange the sliced tomatoes on a plate and place the salad over them. Garnish with the coriander leaves. Refrigerate before serving.

Serves 4-6.

FENNEL SALAD

1/2 cup olive oil
3 cloves garlic, crushed
1 small red onion, thinly
  sliced
1 cup firm tofu, drained,
  cubed
1 large bulb fennel, thinly
  sliced
2 large tomatoes, cut into 6
  wedges
1/2 cup stuffed green olives
1 teaspoon ground fennel
  seeds
1 teaspoon salt
1/2 teaspoon ground black
  pepper
juice of 1 lemon
1/4 cup Italian parsley,
  chopped
4 green onions, chopped

In a large bowl, combine the olive oil, garlic, onion, tofu, fennel, tomatoes, green olives, fennel seeds, salt, pepper, and lemon juice. Mix well and refrigerate. Garnish with the Italian parsley and green onions.

Serves 4-6.

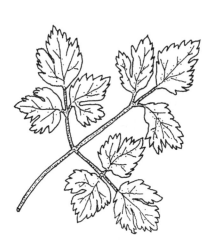

LEBANESE SALAD

1 head green leaf lettuce, washed, drained, cut into 2-inch squares
1 pkg. extra firm tofu (12.4 oz.), drained, cubed
1 cucumber, peeled, cubed
6 radishes, cut into wedges
2 large tomatoes, cubed
1 large green bell pepper, seeded, cubed
1 small red onion, chopped
1/2 cup green onion, chopped
2 tablespoons fresh mint, chopped
1/2 cup fresh Italian parsley, chopped
1/2 cup olive oil
juice of 1 lemon
1 teaspoon salt
1/2 teaspoon ground black pepper
3 cloves garlic, crushed
1/2 teaspoon cayenne powder
2 Pita bread pockets, cubed, toasted
1 teaspoon paprika

In a large salad bowl, arrange the lettuce, tofu, cucumber, radishes, tomatoes, green bell pepper, onion, green onion, mint, and parsley in layers. In a small bowl, mix the olive oil, lemon juice, salt, pepper, garlic, cayenne powder, and toasted Pita bread pockets. Pour the dressing over the salad and toss. Sprinkle with the paprika. Chill before serving.

Serves 4-6.

Lentil Salad

2 cups cooked lentils
4 cloves garlic, crushed
1 pkg. extra firm tofu
  (12.4 oz.), drained, cubed
1 small yellow onion,
  chopped
1/2 cup celery, diced
1/2 cup green onion,
  chopped
1/2 cup Italian parsley,
  chopped
1 teaspoon salt
1/2 teaspoon ground black
  pepper
2 teaspoons ground cumin
1 tablespoon curry powder
juice of 1 lemon
1/4 cup olive oil
1 teaspoon paprika

In a large salad bowl, thoroughly mix the lentils, garlic, tofu, onion, celery, green onion, parsley, salt, pepper, cumin, curry powder, lemon juice, and olive oil. Sprinkle with the paprika. Chill before serving.

Serves 4-6.

MANDARIN ORANGE SALAD

1 head red leaf lettuce, washed, drained, cut into 2-inch squares
1 small red bell pepper, seeded, sliced
1 pkg. extra firm tofu (12.4 oz.), drained, cubed
1 cucumber, peeled, thinly sliced
1 large tomato, thinly sliced
1 small red onion, thinly sliced
2 green onions, finely chopped
1 can whole Mandarin orange segments (11 oz.), drained
1/4 cup slivered almonds, toasted
1/4 cup fresh orange juice
1/4 cup canola oil
2 tablespoons fresh lemon juice
1 teaspoon salt
3 cloves garlic, crushed
1/2 teaspoon ground mustard
1 teaspoon honey

In a large salad bowl, arrange the lettuce leaves, bell pepper, tofu, cucumber, tomato, onion, green onions, Mandarin orange segments, and toasted almonds in layers. In a small bowl, mix the orange juice, canola oil, lemon juice, salt, garlic, mustard and honey. Pour the dressing over the salad and toss. Chill before serving.

Serves 4-6.

Seafood Salad with Tofu

1 pkg. firm tofu (16 oz.),
   drained, cubed
1 cup cooked baby shrimp
1 cup cooked scallops
1/2 cup canned crab meat
1 cup fresh string beans,
   ends removed, cut into
   julienne strips
1 tablespoon fresh tarragon
   leaves
2 tablespoons dill weed
1 teaspoon salt
1/2 teaspoon ground white
   pepper
1/2 teaspoon sugar
   (optional)
1/2 cup olive oil
juice of 1 lime
1/4 cup fresh coriander
   leaves, chopped

In a large salad bowl, arrange the tofu, cooked shrimp, cooked scallops, crab meat, and string beans in layers. In a small bowl, mix the tarragon, dill weed, salt, pepper, sugar, olive oil, and lime juice. Pour the dressing over the salad and toss. Garnish with the coriander leaves. Chill before serving.

Serves 4-6.

SHRIMP SALAD

1 cup cooked elbow
  macaroni
1 cup cooked baby shrimp
1 cup extra firm tofu,
  drained, cubed
1/2 cup celery, chopped
1/2 cup green onion,
  chopped
1 small yellow onion,
  chopped
1/2 cup stuffed green olives,
  chopped
1/2 teaspoon salt
1 cup Tofu Lemon
  Mayonnaise (see page 19)
2 tablespoons fresh
  lemon juice
1/4 cup Italian parsley,
  chopped
1/2 teaspoon ground
  white pepper
1 teaspoon paprika

In a large salad bowl, thoroughly mix the macaroni, shrimp, tofu, celery, green onion, onion, olives, salt, mayonnaise, lemon juice, parsley, and pepper. Sprinkle with the paprika. Chill before serving.

Serves 4-6.

SPINACH SALAD

1 lb. fresh spinach leaves,
   washed, stems removed
1 small red onion, sliced
1 pkg. extra firm tofu
   (12.4 oz.), drained, cubed
1/2 cup bacon bits (optional)
1/2 cup olive oil
3 cloves garlic, crushed
3 tablespoons fresh
   lemon juice
1 teaspoon honey
1/2 teaspoon salt
1 teaspoon dry mustard
1/2 teaspoon ground
   black pepper
3 green onions, chopped
1/2 cup pine nuts

In a large salad bowl, arrange the spinach, red onion, tofu, and bacon bits in layers. In a small bowl, mix the olive oil, garlic, lemon juice, honey, salt, mustard, pepper, and green onions. Pour the dressing over the salad and toss. Garnish with the pine nuts.

Serves 4-6.

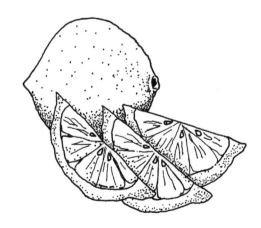

THAI SALAD

1/4 cup fish sauce (Nam Pla)
  or 1/4 cup soy sauce
juice of 2 limes
1 pkg. firm tofu (16 oz.),
  drained, cubed
2 tablespoons sugar
1/2 head of head lettuce,
  cubed
1 large carrot, peeled,
  shredded
1 cucumber, peeled, cut into
  julienne strips
2 fresh red cayenne peppers,
  sliced
1/4 cup fresh basil, chopped
1/4 cup fresh mint, chopped
4 green onions, chopped
1/4 cup fresh coriander,
  chopped
1/4 cup unsalted roasted
  peanuts, crushed

In a large salad bowl, thoroughly mix the fish sauce, lime juice, tofu, sugar, lettuce, carrot, cucumber, cayenne peppers, basil, mint, green onions, and coriander leaves. Garnish with the peanuts before serving.

Serves 4-6.

CHAPTER FIVE

VEGETABLES

Vegetables

EGGPLANT LASAGNA

1/4 cup grated Parmesan
  cheese
1 1/2 cups bread crumbs
1 teaspoon salt
1/2 teaspoon ground black
  pepper
3 eggs, beaten
2 large eggplants, peeled,
  cut into 1/4-inch thick
  slices
1 cup soft tofu, drained,
  mashed
1/2 cup ricotta cheese
1 cup grated mozzarella
  cheese
6 fresh basil leaves, chopped
3 cloves garlic, crushed
1/2 cup Italian parsley,
  chopped
1 egg, beaten (optional)
4 cups Italian Tomato Sauce
  (see page 16)

On a large flat plate, combine the Parmesan cheese, bread crumbs, salt, and pepper. Set aside. On a large plate, place the 3 beaten eggs. Coat both sides of each slice of the eggplant with the 3 beaten eggs and then coat it with the bread crumb mixture. Lay the coated slices on an oiled cookie sheet and bake at 375 degrees for 8 to 10 minutes or until golden brown on both sides. Set aside. In a large bowl, mix the tofu, ricotta cheese, mozzarella, basil leaves, garlic, parsley, and egg. Set aside. In a buttered 9x13 baking dish, arrange in alternate layers the oven-baked eggplant, tofu mixture and Italian Tomato Sauce. Bake the eggplant lasagne at 350 degrees for 30 minutes or until the top is light golden brown.

Serves 4-6.

MEATLESS TOFU BALLS

2 cups firm tofu, drained, crushed
1 egg, beaten (optional)
1 cup whole wheat flour
1 cup bread crumbs
1/2 cup grated Parmesan cheese
1/2 teaspoon brown sugar
1/2 cup Italian parsley, chopped
4 cloves garlic, crushed
4 fresh basil leaves, chopped
1 teaspoon salt
1/2 teaspoon ground black pepper
1/2 cup olive oil for frying
2 cups tomato sauce or Italian Tomato Sauce (see page 16)
2 bay leaves
1/2 cup dry white wine

In a large bowl, combine the tofu, egg, flour, bread crumbs, Parmesan cheese, sugar, Italian parsley, garlic, basil leaves, salt, and pepper. Knead the mixture for 2 minutes or until it holds together. Shape the mixture into 2-inch balls. Fry in olive oil until golden brown all over. Remove and drain on paper towels. Set aside. In a large pot, put the tomato sauce, bay leaves, wine, and fried tofu balls and simmer for 15 minutes. Serve over pasta or rice.

Serves 4-6.

Scrambled Eggs with Tofu

1 cup firm tofu, drained,
  mashed
3 eggs, beaten
1/2 teaspoon salt
1/4 teaspoon ground black
  pepper
2 tablespoons butter or
  margarine
1 small yellow onion, finely
  chopped
1/4 cup green onion,
  chopped
1 teaspoon paprika

In a small bowl, mix the tofu, eggs, salt, and black pepper until smooth. Set aside. Melt the butter in a large frying pan and sauté the onion and green onion until light golden brown. Add the tofu mixture and cover. Cook over medium-low heat for 3 minutes. Uncover and sprinkle with the paprika.

Serves 4.

Spicy Scrambled Eggs

1/2 cup firm tofu, drained,
  mashed
1 small potato, shredded
3 eggs, beaten
1/2 teaspoon salt
1/4 teaspoon cayenne
  powder
2 tablespoons olive oil
3 cloves garlic, crushed
1/4 cup fresh coriander
  leaves, chopped

In a small bowl, mix the tofu, potato, eggs, salt, and cayenne powder until smooth. Set aside. Heat the oil in a large frying pan and sauté the garlic until light golden brown. Add the tofu mixture and cover. Cook over medium-low heat for 3 minutes. Uncover and garnish with the coriander leaves.

Serves 4.

SPICY SWEET AND SOUR TOFU BALLS

Tofu Balls

2 pkgs. extra firm tofu
   (12.4 oz. each), drained,
   mashed
1/2 cup bread crumbs
2 eggs, beaten (optional)
4 water chestnuts, minced
4 cloves garlic, minced
4 green onions, minced
1/2 teaspoon ground
   white pepper
1/2 teaspoon salt
1/2 teaspoon brown sugar
1 tablespoon soy sauce
2 tablespoons cornstarch
1 tablespoon sesame oil
1 cup canola oil for
   deep-frying

Sauce

1 fresh red cayenne pepper,
   sliced
1/2 cup ketchup
1 tablespoon cornstarch
1 cup water
1/4 cup honey
juice of 1 lime
1 red bell pepper, seeded,
   cubed
1 cup canned pineapple
   chunks
1/2 cup roasted cashew
   nuts

In a large bowl, mix the tofu, bread crumbs, eggs, water chestnuts, garlic, green onions, pepper, salt, sugar, soy sauce, cornstarch, and sesame oil. Shape the tofu mixture into 1-inch balls. Heat the oil in a wok and deep-fry the tofu balls until golden brown all over. Remove and drain on paper towels. Set aside. In a large pot, mix the cayenne pepper, ketchup, cornstarch, water, honey, lime juice, bell pepper, and pineapple. Cook over medium heat for 3 minutes, stirring occasionally. Add the fried tofu balls and simmer for 5 minutes. Garnish with the cashew nuts.

Serves 4-6.

Spicy Thai Mixed Vegetables

2 tablespoons canola oil
3 cloves garlic, crushed
1 stalk fresh lemon grass,
  cut into 2-inch lengths
4 fresh red cayenne peppers,
  sliced
4 kaffir lime leaves
1/2 lb. string beans, ends
  removed, cut into 2-inch
  lengths
1 can baby corn (15 oz.),
  drained
1 can straw mushrooms
  (8 oz.), drained
1 cup sliced Japanese
  eggplant
1/2 cup canned shredded
  bamboo shoots
1 pkg. firm tofu (16 oz.),
  drained, cubed
1 cup canned coconut milk
1 teaspoon salt
1/2 teaspoon ground black
  pepper
1/2 cup fresh basil leaves

Heat the oil in a large deep pot and stir-fry the garlic, lemon grass, cayenne peppers, lime leaves, and string beans for 3 minutes. Add the baby corn, straw mushrooms, eggplant, bamboo shoots, tofu, coconut milk, salt, pepper, and basil leaves and simmer for 5 minutes. Serve hot over rice.

Serves 4-6.

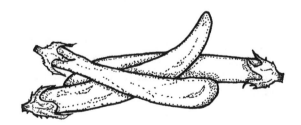

Spinach and Tofu Quiche

Filling

1 cup soft tofu, drained, mashed
1 cup soy bean milk (see page 146) or regular milk
1 tablespoon cornstarch
1 teaspoon salt
1 teaspoon Worcestershire sauce
2 eggs, beaten
1 pkg. chopped frozen spinach (10 oz.), thawed, drained, water squeezed out
2/3 cup grated Swiss cheese

Crust

2 cups flour
1/8 teaspoon salt
1/2 cup butter or margarine
1/4 cup cold water

Combine the tofu, soy milk, cornstarch, salt, Worcestershire sauce, and eggs in a blender and blend until smooth. Pour the mixture into a bowl and add the spinach and half of the grated cheese. Mix well and set aside. In a small bowl, make the crust by thoroughly mixing the flour, salt, butter and cold water into a dough. Refrigerate for about 10 minutes before rolling out. Roll out the dough into an 11-inch circle. Place it in a 9-inch pie pan and pierce the bottom and sides with a fork to prevent the crust from bubbling and losing its shape. Bake in a 350 degree oven for 10 minutes or until the crust is light golden brown. Cool and fill with the spinach mixture. Sprinkle with the remaining cheese on the top. Bake in a 350 degree oven for 30 minutes, or until it begins to puff and is firm in the center. Cool before serving.

Serves 4-6.

STIR-FRIED YUBA

2 tablespoons sesame oil
3 cloves garlic, crushed
1 lb. fresh string beans, ends removed, cut into 2-inch lengths
1 large carrot, peeled, cut into julienne strips
1 small white icicle radish, peeled, cut into julienne strips
6 yuba sticks (dry bean curd), soaked in 2 cups of warm water for 20 minutes, drained, cut into 2-inch lengths
1/2 teaspoon salt
2 tablespoons light soy sauce
4 green onions, chopped

Heat the oil in a wok and sauté the garlic, string beans, carrot, white icicle radish, yuba, and salt for 5 minutes or until the vegetables are soft. Add the soy sauce and simmer for 2 minutes. Garnish with the green onions.

Serves 4-6.

STIR-FRIED YUBA WITH TOFU

2 tablespoons canola oil
1 leek, chopped
1 fresh red cayenne pepper, sliced
6 yuba sticks (dry bean curd), soaked in 2 cups of warm water for 20 minutes, drained, cut into 2-inch lengths
1 pkg. firm tofu (16 oz.), drained, cubed
3 tablespoons soy sauce
1/4 cup fresh coriander leaves, chopped

Heat the oil in a wok and sauté the leek, cayenne, yuba, and tofu for 3 minutes, stirring occasionally. Add the soy sauce and simmer for 2 minutes. Garnish with the coriander leaves.

Serves 4-6.

STUFFED BAKED TOMATOES

8 large firm red tomatoes
1/2 cup extra firm tofu,
  drained
1 cup fresh mushrooms,
  washed, chopped
3 cloves garlic, crushed
2 green onions, chopped
1 small yellow onion,
  chopped
1/2 cup Italian parsley,
  chopped
1 teaspoon salt
1/2 teaspoon ground black
  pepper
1/4 cup bread crumbs
1/4 cup grated Parmesan
  cheese
1 teaspoon paprika

Cut off the tops and core the tomatoes. Rinse them out with water and set aside. In a small bowl, thoroughly mix the tofu, mushrooms, garlic, green onions, onion, parsley, salt, pepper, and bread crumbs. Firmly stuff the mixture into the tomatoes. In an oiled 9x13 inch baking pan, arrange the stuffed tomatoes and sprinkle with the Parmesan cheese and paprika. Bake in a 350 degree oven for 30 minutes or until the top is light golden brown.

Serves 6-8.

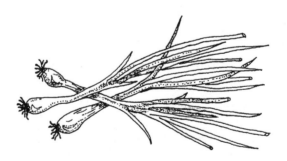

STUFFED EGGPLANT

2 cups water
1 large eggplant
2 tablespoons olive oil
1 small yellow onion,
  chopped
2 cloves garlic, crushed
1 cup fresh mushrooms,
  washed, drained, chopped
1 cup firm tofu, drained,
  mashed
1 teaspoon salt
1/2 teaspoon ground black
  pepper
1/4 cup Italian parsley,
  chopped
1 tablespoon fresh lemon
  juice
1/4 cup bread crumbs
1/4 cup grated Parmesan
  cheese
1 teaspoon paprika

Bring the water to a boil in a deep pot. Put the eggplant into the boiling water for 3 minutes. Drain the water and cut the eggplant in half lengthwise. Remove the eggplant pulp down to about 1/2 inch. Chop and set the pulp aside. Heat the oil in a frying pan and sauté the onion and garlic until light golden brown. Add the chopped eggplant pulp, mushrooms, tofu, salt, pepper, Italian parsley, lemon juice, and bread crumbs. Stuff the eggplant shells with the mixture and place them into an oiled 9x13 inch baking dish and sprinkle with the Parmesan cheese and paprika. Bake the eggplant, uncovered, at 350 degrees for 30 minutes or until the top is golden brown.

Serves 4.

STUFFED ZUCCHINI

4 cups of water
2 green zucchinis, about
   9 to 10 inches long, split
   lengthwise
2 tablespoons canola oil
1 small yellow onion,
   chopped
3 cloves garlic, crushed
1 large carrot, peeled, grated
1 cup soft tofu, drained,
   mashed
1 tablespoon curry powder
1 teaspoon salt
1/2 teaspoon ground white
   pepper
2 tablespoons flour
1/4 cup milk
2 tablespoons grated
   Parmesan cheese
1 teaspoon paprika

Bring the water to a boil in a large deep pot. Add the zucchini halves and boil for 3 minutes. Drain and cool. Scoop out and chop up the pulp from the centers of the halves. Set aside. Heat the oil in a frying pan over medium heat and sauté the onion and garlic until light golden brown. Add the carrot, tofu, curry powder, salt, pepper, flour, and chopped pulp. Sauté for 3 minutes, then add the milk. Stir the mixture until creamy. Fill the four zucchini halves with the mixture and place on a buttered 9x13 baking pan and sprinkle with the Parmesan cheese and paprika. Bake in a 350 degree oven, uncovered, for 30 minutes.

Serves 4-6.

TOFUBURGERS WITH HERBS

1 1/2 cups firm tofu,
   drained, mashed
1/2 cup whole wheat flour
1 teaspoon salt
1/2 teaspoon ground black
   pepper
3 cloves garlic, crushed
1 egg, beaten (optional)
1/4 cup Italian parsley, finely
   chopped
1/4 cup olive oil

In a large bowl, thoroughly mix the tofu, flour, salt, pepper, garlic, egg, parsley, and oil until it has the consistency of ground meat. Shape into patties and either fry or bake them until golden brown on both sides. Serve with rolls or on buns.

Serves 4-6.

TOFUBURGERS WITH YUBA

2 cups firm tofu, drained,
   mashed
1 cup whole wheat flour
3 yuba sticks (dry bean
   curd), soaked in 2 cups
   of warm water for
   20 minutes, drained,
   finely chopped
1 teaspoon salt
3 cloves garlic, crushed
1 egg, beaten
4 green onions, chopped
1/4 cup canola oil

In a large bowl, thoroughly mix the tofu, flour, yuba, salt, garlic, egg, green onions, and oil until it has the consistency of ground meat. Shape into patties and either fry or bake them until golden brown on both sides. Serve with rolls or on buns.

Serves 4-6.

TOFU CHEESE CASSEROLE

2 tablespoons canola oil
1 large yellow onion,
chopped
3 cloves garlic, crushed
2 large potatoes, peeled,
cubed
1 pkg. firm tofu (16 oz.),
drained, cubed
2 tablespoons flour, sifted
1 teaspoon salt
1/2 teaspoon ground white
pepper
1 teaspoon dried thyme
1/2 cup Italian parsley,
finely chopped
1 cup milk
1 cup shredded Swiss
cheese
1/2 cup bread crumbs
4 green onions, chopped
1/2 cup Parmesan cheese
1 teaspoon paprika

Heat the oil in a large pot and sauté the onion and garlic until light golden brown. Add the potatoes and sauté for 3 minutes, stirring occasionally. Add the tofu, flour, salt, pepper, thyme, parsley, and milk. Simmer for 2 minutes. Pour the tofu mixture into a large buttered 9x13 inch baking pan. Sprinkle with the Swiss cheese, bread crumbs, green onions, Parmesan cheese, and paprika. Cover and bake in a 350 degree oven for 30 minutes or until the potatoes are tender.

Serves 4-6.

TOFU RATATOUILLE

1/4 cup olive oil
1 large yellow onion,
chopped
4 cloves garlic, crushed
1 large eggplant, cubed
2 red bell peppers, seeded,
cubed
1 zucchini, cubed
1 summer squash, cubed
2 large tomatoes, peeled,
cubed
1 extra firm tofu (12.4 oz.),
drained, cubed
1 bay leaf
1/2 teaspoon fresh oregano
1 teaspoon dill weed
2 tablespoons dry white
wine
1 fresh red cayenne pepper
(optional)
1 cup tomato juice
1/4 cup tomato paste
1 teaspoon salt
2 fresh basil leaves
1/2 teaspoon ground black
pepper
1/4 cup Italian parsley,
chopped
1/4 cup grated Parmesan
cheese

Heat the oil in a large deep pot and sauté the onion and garlic until light golden brown. Add the eggplant, bell pepper, zucchini and summer squash. Sauté for 3 minutes and add the tomatoes, tofu, bay leaf, oregano, dill weed, wine, cayenne pepper, tomato juice, tomato paste, salt, basil leaves, and pepper. Cover and simmer for 15 minutes or until the vegetables are tender. Garnish with the Italian parsley and Parmesan cheese.

Serves 4-6.

TOFU SOUFFLÉ

1 carrot, peeled, chopped
1 cup soft tofu, drained,
  mashed
1/2 cup soy bean milk
  (see page 146) or
  regular milk
1/2 teaspoon salt
1/2 teaspoon ground white
  pepper
1 teaspoon dill weed
1/4 teaspoon dry mustard
1 tablespoon butter or
  margarine, melted
1/4 cup green onion,
  chopped
1/4 cup grated Parmesan
  cheese
6 tablespoons bread crumbs
3 eggs, separated, at room
  temperature
2 tablespoons grated
  Swiss cheese

In a blender, blend the carrot, tofu, soy milk, salt, pepper, dill weed, mustard, butter, green onion, Parmesan cheese, bread crumbs, and egg yolks until very smooth. Pour the mixture into a bowl and fold in stiffly beaten egg whites. Pour into a buttered 1 1/2-quart soufflé dish. Sprinkle with the Swiss cheese and bake, uncovered, in a 375 degree oven for 30-40 minutes or until the top is golden brown.

Serves 4-6.

TOFU TAMALE PIE

2 tablespoons canola oil
1 small yellow onion, chopped
4 cloves garlic, crushed
1 large red bell pepper, seeded, chopped
1 cup soft tofu, drained, mashed
1 cup canned whole tomatoes, chopped
1 cup black olives, pitted, chopped
2 cups canned whole corn
3/4 cup soy bean milk (see page 146) or regular milk
1 tablespoon chili powder
1 tablespoon cumin powder
1 teaspoon coriander powder
1 teaspoon salt
1 cup corn meal
1 teaspoon cayenne powder (optional)
1/4 cup fresh coriander leaves, chopped
1 cup grated cheddar cheese

Heat the oil in a large frying pan and sauté the onion and garlic until light golden brown. Add the bell pepper and sauté for 2 minutes. Pour this mixture into a large bowl and mix in the tofu, tomatoes, olives, corn, milk, chili, cumin, coriander powder, salt, corn meal, cayenne powder, and coriander leaves. Pour the tamale mixture into a 9x13 inch baking pan and bake, uncovered, in a 350 degree oven for 45 minutes or until the top is light brown. Remove from the oven and sprinkle with the cheddar cheese and return it to the oven for an additional 10 minutes.

Serves 4-6.

Tofu with Black Bean Sauce

2 tablespoons canola oil
3 cloves garlic, crushed
1 teaspoon finely grated ginger
2 tablespoons salted black beans (Chinese style)
1 leek, thinly sliced
1 fresh red cayenne pepper, sliced
2 cups firm tofu, drained, cubed
1 tablespoon soy sauce
1 tablespoon cornstarch, dissolved in 1/4 cup of cold water
1 tablespoon sesame oil
4 green onions, chopped

Heat the oil in a wok and sauté the garlic, ginger, and salted black beans for 1 minute. Add the leek, cayenne pepper, tofu, soy sauce, and cornstarch mixture. Stir and simmer for 3 minutes. Sprinkle with the sesame oil and garnish with the green onions.

Serves 4-6.

Tofu with Green Beans

2 tablespoons canola oil
3 cloves garlic, crushed
1 lb. fresh green beans, ends removed, cut into 2-inch lengths
1 cup firm tofu, drained, cubed
1 tablespoon fresh lemon juice
1/2 teaspoon salt
1/4 cup walnuts, chopped

Heat the oil in a wok and sauté the garlic and green beans for 3 minutes. Add the tofu, lemon juice, and salt and simmer for 5 minutes. Sprinkle with the walnuts.

Serves 4-6.

VEGETABLE TOFU CURRY

2 tablespoons canola oil
3 cloves garlic, crushed
1 small yellow onion,
  chopped
1 tablespoon fresh grated
  ginger
1 lb. eggplant, cut into
  2-inch cubes
1 large red bell pepper,
  seeded, cubed
1 large carrot, peeled, sliced
1 lb. string beans, ends
  removed, cut into 2-inch
  lengths
1 pkg. extra firm tofu
  (12.4 oz.), drained, cubed
2 large tomatoes, chopped
1 tablespoon ground cumin
1 tablespoon ground
  coriander
1 teaspoon turmeric
2 fresh red cayenne peppers,
  sliced
1/2 teaspoon salt
4 kaffir lime leaves
juice of 1 lime
2 cups plain yogurt
1/4 cup fresh coriander
  leaves, chopped

Heat the oil in a large pot and sauté the garlic, onion, and ginger until light golden brown. Add the eggplant, bell pepper, carrot, string beans, tofu, tomatoes, cumin, coriander, turmeric, cayenne peppers, salt, kaffir lime leaves, and lime juice. Cover and simmer for 10 minutes or until the vegetables are soft. Do not overcook the vegetables. Add the yogurt and simmer for 2 minutes. Garnish with the coriander leaves.

Serves 4-6.

VEGETABLES WITH SPICY PEANUT SAUCE

1 pkg. firm tofu (16 oz.), drained, cut into 1-inch cubes

1/2 cup canola oil for deep-frying

2 large carrots, peeled, boiled, cubed

2 large potatoes, peeled, boiled, cubed

1 lb. string beans, ends removed, boiled, cut into 2-inch lengths

1 small green cabbage, boiled, cubed

1 cucumber, peeled, sliced

2 hard boiled eggs, sliced

1 lb. fresh bean sprouts, blanched

3 cups Spicy Peanut Sauce (see page 18)

1 cup fresh coriander leaves, chopped

Heat the oil in a wok and fry the tofu until golden brown on both sides. Remove and drain on paper towels. Set aside. In a large salad bowl, arrange the fried tofu, carrots, potatoes, string beans, cabbage, cucumber, hard boiled eggs, and bean sprouts in layers. Pour the Spicy Peanut Sauce over the vegetables and toss just before serving. Garnish with the coriander leaves.

Serves 4-6.

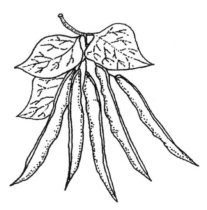

CHAPTER SIX

SEAFOOD

Seafood

CRAB SOUFFLÉ

2 cups soft tofu, drained,
  mashed
1 cup milk
1/2 teaspoon salt
1/2 teaspoon ground white
  pepper
1 small yellow onion, sliced
1 tablespoon butter or
  margarine, melted
2 tablespoons Italian
  parsley, chopped
1/4 cup bread crumbs
1/4 cup flour
4 cups eggs, separated
1 cup canned crab meat
1/2 cup grated Swiss cheese
1/4 cup grated Parmesan
  cheese

In a blender, blend the tofu, milk, salt, pepper, onion, butter, parsley, bread crumbs, flour, and egg yolks until very smooth. Pour the mixture into a large bowl and add the crab meat and Swiss cheese. Thoroughly mix and gently fold in stiffly beaten egg whites. Pour into a buttered 1½ quart soufflé dish. Sprinkle with the Parmesan cheese and bake in a 375 degree oven for 30-40 minutes or until the top is golden brown.

Serves 4-6.

Stuffed Nori with Crab

1 pkg. firm tofu (16 oz.),
  drained, mashed
1 lb. medium shrimp,
  shelled, deveined
  (see diagram, page 149),
  finely chopped
1 cup canned crab meat
1/2 cup green onion,
  chopped
3 cloves garlic, crushed
1 teaspoon salt
1/2 teaspoon ground white
  pepper
1 tablespoon sesame oil
1 egg, beaten (optional)
6 sheets of nori (seaweed
  sheets)
2 cups canola oil for
  deep-frying

In a large bowl, thoroughly mix the tofu, shrimp, crab meat, green onion, garlic, salt, pepper, sesame oil, and egg. Divide the tofu mixture into 6 portions and spread each evenly along one end of each nori sheet and roll up the nori tightly. Heat the oil in a large wok and deep-fry the stuffed nori rolls until crispy and golden brown. Cool and cut each roll in 1-inch slices with a very sharp knife. Serve with Hot Sweet Sauce (see page 15).

Serves 4-6.

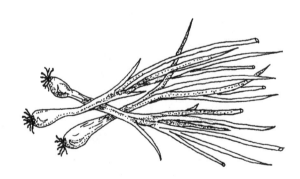

Dried Cod Fish with Tofu

1 lb. dried cod fish
2 tablespoons white flour
2 tablespoons canola oil
3 cloves garlic, crushed
1 pkg. firm tofu, drained, cubed
1 fresh red cayenne pepper, sliced (optional)
2 large tomatoes, chopped
1 teaspoon brown sugar
4 green onions, cut into 2-inch lengths
1/4 cup fresh coriander leaves, chopped

In a small bowl, soak the cod fish in water overnight. Drain, remove skin and bones, and cut into 2-inch squares. Coat the cod fish squares with flour and set aside for 5 minutes. Heat the oil in a wok and sauté the garlic and cod fish until brown. Add the tofu, cayenne pepper, tomatoes, sugar, and green onions. Sauté for 2 more minutes and garnish with the coriander leaves.

Servers 4-6.

STUFFED BAKED FISH WITH TOFU

1 whole red snapper
  or grouper (3-4 lbs.)
juice of 2 lemons
1 teaspoon salt
1/2 cup cooked baby shrimp
3 cloves garlic, crushed
1 cup firm tofu, drained,
  mashed
2 green onions, minced
1/4 cup Italian parsley,
  chopped
1/2 teaspoon ground white
  pepper
2 slices of bread, cut into
  1-inch cubes
1/4 cup olive oil
1/4 cup dry white wine
4 green onions, chopped

Place the fish in a large bowl and rub with the lemon juice and salt. Set aside. In a small bowl, mix the shrimp, garlic, tofu, green onions, Italian parsley, pepper and bread. Stuff the fish with the shrimp and tofu mixture and place it in a buttered baking dish. Brush the fish with the olive oil and pour the wine over it. Bake in a 375 degree oven for 40 minutes or until the fish is cooked. Garnish with the green onions.

Serves 4-6.

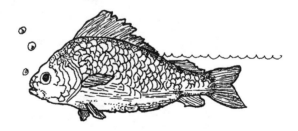

JAMBALAYA SHRIMP

1/4 cup olive oil
1 pkg. firm tofu (16 oz.),
  drained, cut into 1/2-inch
  thick slices
2 tablespoons butter or
  margarine
1 large yellow onion,
  chopped
1 cup fresh mushrooms,
  washed, drained, sliced
3 cloves garlic, crushed
1 green bell pepper, seeded,
  cubed
1 red bell pepper, seeded,
  cubed
1 stalk celery, chopped
2 large red tomatoes, peeled,
  seeded, chopped
1 cup cooked baby shrimp
1 fresh red cayenne pepper
  (optional)
1 bay leaf
1 teaspoon salt
1/2 teaspoon ground black
  pepper
1 teaspoon thyme
1/2 cup Italian parsley,
  chopped

Heat the oil in a large frying pan and fry the tofu until crispy and golden brown on both sides. Remove and drain on paper towels. Cool and cut the slices into 1-inch cubes. Set the tofu cubes aside. Melt the butter in a large pot and sauté the onion until golden brown. Add the mushrooms, garlic, green pepper, red pepper, celery, tomatoes, shrimp, cayenne pepper, bay leaf, salt, pepper, thyme, parsley and fried tofu. Simmer for 15 minutes. Serve over white or brown rice.

Serves 4-6.

SHRIMP AND TOFU CREOLE

1/4 cup olive oil
2 pkgs. extra firm tofu
(12.4 oz. each), drained,
cubed
1 cup cooked baby shrimp
1 small yellow onion,
chopped
3 cloves garlic, crushed
1 red bell pepper, seeded,
chopped
1 green bell pepper, seeded,
chopped
4 cups canned whole
tomatoes, drained,
chopped
1/2 cup tomato sauce
2 bay leaves
1 fresh red cayenne pepper,
sliced
1 teaspoon salt
1 cup canned whole okra,
drained
1/4 cup fresh coriander
leaves, chopped

Heat the oil in a large pot. Fry the tofu until golden brown on both sides. Remove and drain on paper towels. Set aside. In the same large pot, sauté the shrimp, onion and garlic for 2 minutes. Add the red bell pepper, green bell pepper, tomatoes, tomato sauce, bay leaves, cayenne pepper, salt, okra and fried tofu. Lower the heat and simmer for 20 minutes. Garnish with the coriander leaves. Serve over rice.

Serves 4-6.

SHRIMP SCAMPI CASSEROLE

3 tablespoons butter
  or margarine
3 cloves garlic, chopped
1 cup firm tofu, drained,
  cubed
2 lbs. large shrimp, shelled,
  deveined (see diagram,
  page149)
1/4 cup Italian parsley,
  chopped
1/4 cup green onion,
  chopped
1/2 teaspoon salt
1/2 teaspoon ground white
  pepper
2 tablespoons bread crumbs
3 tablespoons grated
  Parmesan cheese
1 teaspoon paprika

Melt the butter in a large pot and sauté the garlic and tofu until light golden brown. Add the shrimp, parsley, green onion, salt and pepper and sauté for 3 more minutes. Place the tofu and shrimp mixture in a large buttered 9x13 inch baking pan and sprinkle with the bread crumbs, Parmesan cheese, and paprika. Bake in a 450 degree oven for 10 minutes or until the top is light brown.

Serves 4-6.

STIR-FRIED SHRIMP AND SQUID

3 tablespoons canola oil
1 small yellow onion, sliced
3 cloves garlic, crushed
1/2 lb. large shrimp, shelled,
  deveined (see diagram,
  page 149)
1/2 lb. squid, cleaned
  (see diagram, page 147)
1 pkg. extra firm tofu
  (12.4 oz.), drained, cubed
3 tablespoons oyster sauce
4 green onions, chopped

Heat the oil in a large wok and sauté the onion and garlic until light golden brown. Add the shrimp and squid and sauté for 5 minutes, stirring occasionally. Add the tofu, oyster sauce and green onions and sauté for 2 more minutes.

Serves 4-6.

STIR-FRIED SHRIMP AND TOFU

1 lb. large shrimp, shelled, deveined (see diagram, page 149)
1/2 teaspoon salt
1/4 teaspoon ground white pepper
3 tablespoons cornstarch
1 egg white, beaten
1/4 cup canola oil for frying
1 pkg. firm tofu (16 oz.), drained, cubed
3 tablespoons sesame oil
3 cloves garlic, crushed
1 teaspoon fresh ginger, minced
1/2 lb. snow pea pods, ends removed, washed, drained
1/2 lb. fresh mushrooms, washed, drained, sliced
1 fresh red cayenne pepper, sliced
2 tablespoons soy sauce
1 teaspoon sugar
2 green onions, cut into 1-inch lengths

In a small bowl, mix the shrimp, salt, pepper, cornstarch, and egg white. Set aside. Heat the oil in a wok and fry the tofu until golden brown on both sides. Remove and drain on paper towels. Set aside. Heat the sesame oil in a large frying pan and sauté the garlic and ginger until light golden brown. Add the shrimp mixture and stir-fry for 3 minutes. Remove and set aside. In the same frying pan, stir-fry the pea pods, mushrooms, fried tofu, cayenne pepper, soy sauce, sugar and green onions for 2 minutes or until the vegetables are done. Do not overcook. Add the cooked shrimp and stir well. Serve hot over rice.

Serves 4-6.

THAI SHRIMP WITH LEMON GRASS

2 tablespoons canola oil
4 cloves garlic, crushed
1 large red onion, sliced
1 stalk lemon grass, cut
 into 2-inch lengths
2 lbs. large shrimp, shelled,
 deveined (see diagram,
 page 149)
1 cup firm tofu, drained,
 cubed
1 teaspoon salt
2 fresh red cayenne peppers,
 thinly sliced

Heat the oil in a large wok and sauté the garlic, onion, and lemon grass until light golden brown. Add the shrimp and stir-fry for 3 minutes, stirring occasionally. Add the tofu, salt, and cayenne peppers and stir-fry for 2 more minutes.

Serves 4-6.

THAI SHRIMP WITH TOFU

2 tablespoons canola oil
4 cloves garlic, crushed
1 lb. large shrimp, shelled,
 deveined (see diagram,
 page 149)
1 pkg. firm tofu (16 oz.),
 drained, cubed
1 can coconut milk
 (14 fl. oz.)
4 kaffir lime leaves
1 fresh red cayenne pepper,
 thinly sliced
2 tablespoons fish sauce
 (Nam Pla)
1/4 cup fresh coriander
 leaves, chopped

Heat the oil in a wok and sauté the garlic until light golden brown. Add the shrimp, tofu, coconut milk, kaffir lime leaves, cayenne pepper and fish sauce. Cook over medium-low heat for about 10 minutes or until shrimp are cooked. Garnish with the coriander leaves.

Serves 4-6.

THAI SWEET AND SOUR SHRIMP

2 lbs. large shrimp, shelled,
  deveined (see diagram,
  page 149)
1 teaspoon salt
1/2 teaspoon ground white
  pepper
juice of 1 lime
1 tablespoon dry white wine
3 tablespoons canola oil
4 cloves garlic, crushed
1 small red onion, cut into
  2-inch squares
2 fresh red cayenne peppers,
  sliced (optional)
1 large red bell pepper,
  seeded, cut into 1-inch
  squares
1 cup firm tofu, drained,
  cubed
1 tablespoon brown sugar
3 tablespoons tomato paste
1 cup water
1/4 cup canned pineapple
  chunks
2 tablespoons cornstarch,
  dissolved in 1 tablespoon
  cold water
1/4 cup fresh coriander
  leaves, chopped

In a small bowl, season the shrimp with salt, pepper, lime juice, and wine. Marinate for 5 minutes in a refrigerator. Heat the oil in a large wok and sauté the garlic, onion and cayenne peppers until light golden brown. Add the shrimp mixture and sauté for 3 more minutes. Add the red bell pepper, tofu, sugar, tomato paste, water, and pineapple. Stir well and simmer for 3 minutes. Slowly add the cornstarch mixture and stir well. Simmer for 2 more minutes and garnish with the coriander leaves.

Serves 4-6.

CHAPTER SEVEN

MEAT
&
POULTRY

CHAPTER SEVEN
Meat and Poultry

CURRIED BEEF LIVER WITH TOFU

2 tablespoons canola oil
4 cloves garlic, crushed
1 lb. beef liver, thinly sliced,
coated with 2 tablespoons
cornstarch
1 teaspoon salt
1 tablespoon curry powder
1 fresh red cayenne pepper,
thinly sliced
1 pkg. firm tofu (16 oz.),
frozen, thawed, drained,
cubed
4 green onions, cut into
2-inch lengths

Heat the oil in a large wok and sauté the garlic until light golden brown. Add the coated sliced liver, salt and curry powder and stir-fry for 3 minutes. Add the cayenne pepper, tofu and green onions and simmer for 2 minutes until just cooked. Do not overcook.

Serves 4-6.

CURRIED BEEF WITH TOFU

2 tablespoons canola oil
4 cloves garlic, crushed
1 lb. tenderloin beef, sliced
1 large carrot, peeled, sliced
1 teaspoon salt
1 tablespoon curry powder
1 cup firm tofu, drained,
cubed
1/4 cup fresh coriander
leaves, chopped

Heat the oil in a large pot and sauté the garlic until light golden brown. Add the beef, carrot, salt, curry powder, and tofu. Simmer for 10 minutes or until the carrot is soft. Garnish with the coriander leaves.

Serves 4-6.

FRIED TOFU WITH BEEF

1/2 lb. tenderloin beef,
   thinly sliced
3 cloves garlic, crushed
1/2 teaspoon salt
1/4 teaspoon ground white
   pepper
3 tablespoons cornstarch
1/2 cup canola oil for
   deep-frying
1 pkg. firm tofu (16 oz.),
   drained, cubed
3 tablespoons sesame oil
1 fresh red cayenne pepper,
   thinly sliced
2 teaspoons chopped fresh
   ginger
1 cup canned baby corn
1 large carrot, peeled,
   thinly sliced
2 tablespoons oyster sauce
4 green onions, cut into
   2-inch lengths
1/4 cup fresh coriander
   leaves, chopped

In a small bowl, mix the beef, garlic, salt, pepper and cornstarch. Set aside. Heat the canola oil in a wok and deep-fry the tofu until golden brown on both sides. Remove and drain on paper towels. Set aside. Heat the sesame oil in a large frying pan and sauté the cayenne pepper and ginger until light brown. Add the beef mixture and sauté for 3 minutes. Add the fried tofu, baby corn, carrot, oyster sauce, and green onions and sauté for 2 more minutes. Serve hot over rice. Garnish with the coriander leaves.

Serves 4-6.

GINGER BEEF WITH TOFU

2 tablespoons canola oil
1 stalk fresh lemon grass,
    cut into 2-inch lengths
1 tablespoon shredded fresh
    ginger
1 lb. top sirloin beef, thinly
    sliced
3 fresh red cayenne peppers,
    thinly sliced
1 teaspoon salt
1 pkg. firm tofu (16 oz.),
    drained, cubed
1 cup canned coconut milk
1/4 cup fresh coriander
    leaves, chopped

Heat the oil in a large pot and stir-fry the lemon grass, ginger, beef and cayenne peppers for 3 minutes. Add the salt, tofu, coconut milk and simmer for 5 minutes or until the beef is cooked. Garnish with the coriander leaves.

Serves 4-6.

TOFU AND BEEF WITH BASIL

1/2 lb. top sirloin beef,
    thinly sliced
2 tablespoons cornstarch
2 tablespoons canola oil
4 cloves garlic, crushed
4 kaffir lime leaves
1 can straw mushrooms
    (8 oz.), drained
1/2 cup canned shredded
    bamboo shoots
1 pkg. firm tofu (16 oz.),
    drained, cubed
3 fresh red cayenne peppers,
    thinly sliced
1/4 cup oyster sauce
12 sweet basil leaves

In a small bowl, coat the sliced beef with cornstarch on both sides. Set aside. Heat the oil in a wok and sauté the garlic until light golden brown. Add the coated beef and lime leaves and sauté for 3 minutes. Add the mushrooms, bamboo shoots, tofu, cayenne peppers, and oyster sauce. Stir-fry for 2 minutes, mixing in the basil. Serve hot over rice.

Serves 4-6.

TOFU MEAT BALLS

1 lb. lean ground beef
(optional)
1 1/2 cups firm tofu,
drained, mashed
3 cloves garlic, crushed
1 small yellow onion, finely
chopped
1/4 cup Italian parsley,
chopped
1/2 cup walnuts, finely
chopped
1/2 teaspoon salt
1/2 teaspoon ground black
pepper
1 egg, beaten
1/2 cup bread crumbs
1/2 cup olive oil for
deep-frying
2 cups tomato sauce
2 bay leaves
1/2 cup dry white wine

In a large bowl, thoroughly mix the beef, tofu, garlic, onion, Italian parsley, walnuts, salt, pepper, egg, and bread crumbs. Shape into 2-inch balls and deep-fry the meat balls in olive oil until both sides are golden brown. Remove and drain on paper towels. Set aside. Put the tomato sauce, bay leaves and wine in a deep pot and add the fried tofu meat balls. Simmer for 20 minutes. Serve over rice or pasta.

Serves 4-6.

TOFU MEAT LOAF

3 cloves garlic, crushed
1 small yellow onion,
chopped
1 lb. lean ground beef
1/2 lb. lean ground pork
1 cup firm tofu, drained,
mashed
1 teaspoon salt
1/2 teaspoon ground black
pepper
1/2 cup bread crumbs
2 eggs, beaten
1/2 cup celery, chopped
1/2 cup Italian parsley,
chopped
1 tablespoon whole fennel
seeds
1 cup canned tomato sauce
2 tablespoons grated
Parmesan cheese

In a large bowl, thoroughly mix the garlic, onion, ground beef, ground pork, tofu, salt, pepper, bread crumbs, eggs, celery, parsley, and fennel seeds. Shape into a loaf and place in an oiled 9x13 inch baking pan. Bake, covered, in a 350 degree oven for 40 minutes or until the meat is cooked. Pour the tomato sauce over the meat loaf and sprinkle with the Parmesan cheese and bake, uncovered, for 10 more minutes.

Serves 4-6.

TOFU MOUSSAKA

2 tablespoons olive oil
1 small yellow onion, chopped
3 cloves garlic, crushed
1 1/2 lbs. lean ground beef or lamb
2 cups cubed pumpkin
1 teaspoon dried oregano
1/2 teaspoon ground cinnamon
1/2 teaspoon ground ginger
1 teaspoon salt
1/2 teaspoon ground black pepper
1/2 cup Italian parsley, chopped
1 cup cottage cheese
1 egg (optional)
1 cup soft tofu, drained, mashed
2 cups tomato sauce
1/2 cup grated Parmesan cheese

Heat the oil in a large deep pot and sauté the onion and garlic until golden brown. Add the ground beef and sauté for 3 minutes, stirring occasionally. Add the pumpkin, oregano, cinnamon, ginger, salt, and pepper and sauté for 2 minutes. Set aside. In a large bowl, mix the parsley, cottage cheese, egg and tofu. Set aside. In a buttered and floured 9x13 inch baking pan, arrange alternately the pumpkin mixture, cottage cheese mixture, tomato sauce and Parmesan cheese in layers. Repeat the process until all the mixture is used, making sure that the top layer is tomato sauce and Parmesan cheese. Bake in a 350 degree oven for 30 minutes or until the top is brown.

Serves 4-6.

TOFU SPICY BEEF

2 tablespoons canola oil
4 cloves garlic, crushed
1 lb. top sirloin beef, sliced
3 fresh red cayenne
  peppers, sliced
1 cup firm tofu, drained,
  cubed
1 teaspoon salt
4 kaffir lime leaves
1/4 cup fresh coriander
  leaves, chopped

Heat the oil in large wok and sauté the garlic, beef and cayenne peppers for 3 minutes, stirring occasionally. Add the tofu, salt and lime leaves and sauté for 2 minutes. Garnish with the coriander leaves.

Serves 4-6.

TOFU STROGANOFF

2 tablespoons butter or
  margarine
1 small yellow onion, finely
  chopped
1 lb. beef tenderloin, thinly
  sliced (optional)
1 pkg. firm tofu (14.2 oz.),
  drained, cubed
1 teaspoon salt
1 lb. fresh mushrooms,
  washed, drained, sliced
1/2 teaspoon ground white
  pepper
3 tablespoons ketchup
1/4 cup cognac or brandy
2 cups sour cream

Melt the butter in a deep pot and sauté the onion until light golden brown. Add the beef and stir-fry for 3 minutes, stirring occasionally. Add the tofu, salt, and mushrooms. Simmer for about 10 minutes over low heat. Add the pepper, ketchup, cognac and sour cream and simmer again for 2 minutes. Serve over white or brown rice.

Serves 4-6.

BLACK BEANS WITH PORK AND TOFU

2 tablespoons canola oil
1/4 cup green onion, finely
    chopped
1/4 inch piece fresh ginger,
    finely chopped
1/4 lb. extra lean ground
    pork
2 tablespoons salted black
    beans (Chinese style)
1 tablespoon soy sauce
1 fresh red cayenne pepper,
    sliced (optional)
1 teaspoon sugar
1 pkg. firm tofu (16 oz.),
    drained, cubed
4 green onions, chopped
1/4 cup fresh coriander
    leaves

Heat the oil in a wok and sauté the green onion and ginger until light golden brown. Add the pork and black beans and sauté for 2 minutes or until the pork is cooked. Add the soy sauce, cayenne pepper, sugar, and tofu. Simmer for 5 minutes. Garnish with the green onions and coriander leaves. Serve hot over rice.

Serves 4-6.

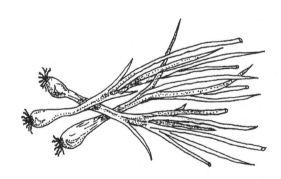

Ma Po Tofu

2 tablespoons canola oil
3 cloves garlic, crushed
1/4 lb. lean ground pork
1/4 teaspoon ground white
  pepper
1/2 teaspoon salt
2 tablespoons soy sauce
2 fresh red cayenne peppers,
  finely chopped (optional)
1 pkg. firm tofu (16 oz.),
  drained, cubed
4 green onions, minced
1 tablespoon cornstarch,
  dissolved in 1/4 cup
  of cold water
1 tablespoon sesame oil
1/4 cup fresh coriander
  leaves, chopped

Heat the oil in a large frying pan and sauté the garlic until light golden brown. Add the pork, pepper, salt and stir-fry for 2 minutes. Add the soy sauce, cayenne peppers and tofu and simmer for 5 minutes. Add the green onions, cornstarch mixture, and sesame oil and cook over low heat, stirring constantly, until the sauce thickens. Garnish with the coriander leaves. Serve hot over rice.

Serves 4-6.

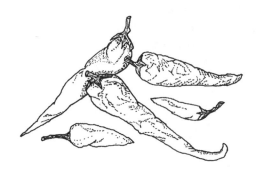

PORK WITH BLACK MUSHROOMS

1/2 lb. tenderloin pork, thinly
   sliced
2 tablespoons cornstarch
2 tablespoons oyster sauce
3 tablespoons canola oil
1/4 inch piece of fresh
   ginger, thinly sliced
3 cloves garlic, crushed
4 dried black Chinese
   mushrooms, soaked in
   1/4 cup of warm water for
   10 minutes (reserve the
   water), cut into julienne
   strips (Note: Remove the
   hard ends from the stems.)
1 pkg. firm tofu (16 oz.),
   drained, cubed
1/2 cup canned sliced
   bamboo shoots
1/2 teaspoon salt
1/2 teaspoon ground white
   pepper
1 teaspoon sesame oil
4 green onions, chopped
1/4 cup fresh coriander
   leaves, chopped

In a small bowl, mix the pork, cornstarch and oyster sauce. Set aside. Heat the oil in a wok and sauté the ginger and garlic until light golden brown. Add the marinated pork and soaked Chinese black mushrooms and sauté for 3 minutes, stirring occasionally. Add the reserved mushroom water, tofu, bamboo shoots, salt, and pepper. Simmer for 5 minutes. Sprinkle with the sesame oil. Garnish with the green onions and coriander leaves. Serve hot over rice.

Serves 4-6.

Stuffed Bell Peppers

1/2 lb. lean ground pork
1 cup cooked brown or
white rice
1/2 cup firm tofu, drained,
mashed
1/2 teaspoon salt
1 small yellow onion,
chopped
2 green onions, chopped
3 cloves garlic, crushed
1/2 teaspoon ground black
pepper
1 teaspoon dried basil
1 egg, beaten
4 large green bell peppers,
seeded, cut lengthwise
1 can tomato sauce (15 oz.)

In a large bowl, mix the pork, rice, tofu, salt, onion, green onions, garlic, pepper, basil, and egg. Stuff the peppers with the mixture and place into an oiled 9x13 inch baking pan and pour the tomato sauce over the peppers. Preheat the oven at 350 degrees for 5 minutes. Then bake the peppers, covered, at 350 degrees for 30 minutes or until peppers are cooked.

Serves 6-8.

STUFFED TOFU

1 pkg. firm tofu (16 oz.),
  drained, cut into 1 1/2-inch
  cubes
1/4 lb. lean ground pork or
  1/4 cup firm tofu, drained,
  mashed
4 cloves garlic, finely
  chopped
3 green onions, minced
2 tablespoons fresh
  coriander leaves, chopped
2 fresh red cayenne peppers,
  chopped (optional)
1/2 teaspoon salt
1/4 teaspoon ground white
  pepper
1 tablespoon cornstarch
1 1/2 cups canola oil for
  deep-frying
Spicy Peanut Sauce
  (see page 18)

Make a 1/2-inch hole in each tofu cube with a small teaspoon. Set aside. Reserve the tofu pulp. In a large bowl, mix the tofu pulp, pork, garlic, green onions, coriander, cayenne peppers, salt, pepper, and cornstarch. Stuff the pork tofu mixture into the hole. Heat the oil in a wok and deep-fry the stuffed tofu until golden brown. Remove and drain on paper towels. Serve with Spicy Peanut Sauce (see page 18).

Serves 4.

CHICKEN BREAST WITH TOFU

1 lb. boneless chicken
breast, thinly sliced
2 tablespoons cornstarch
1 tablespoon soy sauce
3 tablespoons canola oil
3 cloves garlic, crushed
1 pkg. firm tofu (16 oz.),
drained, cubed
2 tablespoons oyster sauce
4 whole dried red cayenne
peppers
10 green onions, cut into
1-inch lengths
1/2 cup unsalted roasted
cashew nuts
1/4 cup fresh coriander
leaves, chopped

In a small bowl, mix the chicken, cornstarch and soy sauce. Set aside. Heat the oil in a wok and sauté the garlic until light golden brown. Add the chicken mixture and sauté for 3 minutes or until the chicken is tender. Add the tofu and sauté for 2 minutes. Add the oyster sauce, cayenne peppers, green onions, and cashew nuts and stir-fry over high heat for 1 minute. Garnish with the coriander leaves. Serve hot over rice.

Serves 4-6.

CHICKEN WITH CASHEW NUTS

1/2 cup canola oil for
deep-frying
1 pkg. firm tofu (16 oz.),
drained, cubed
3 tablespoons canola oil
3 cloves garlic, crushed
1 lb. boneless chicken
breast, cubed, coated with
2 tablespoons cornstarch
4 fresh red cayenne peppers,
sliced (optional)
4 kaffir lime leaves
1 teaspoon salt
6 green onions, cut into
2-inch lengths
1 cup unsalted roasted
cashew nuts
1/4 cup fresh coriander
leaves, chopped

Heat the oil in a wok and
deep-fry the tofu until golden
brown on both sides. Remove
and drain on paper towels. Set
aside. Heat the 3 tablespoons of
oil in a large frying pan and sauté
the garlic, chicken, cayenne
peppers, lime leaves, and salt for
3 minutes or until the chicken is
cooked. Add the fried tofu, green
onions and cashew nuts and
stir-fry for 1 minute. Garnish with
the coriander leaves.

Serves 4-6.

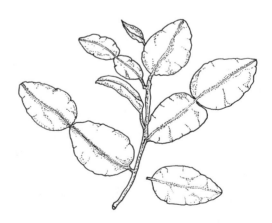

RICE
&
NOODLES

Rice and Noodles

CHINESE FRIED RICE

2 tablespoons canola oil
3 cloves garlic, crushed
1 small yellow onion,
   finely chopped
1 pkg. extra firm tofu
   (12.4 oz.), drained, cut
   into 1/2-inch cubes
1 cup mushrooms, washed,
   drained, thinly sliced
1 small leek, finely chopped
4 cups cooked white or
   brown rice
2 tablespoons soy sauce
1/2 teaspoon salt
1 tablespoon toasted
   sesame seeds
1/2 teaspoon ground white
   pepper
1/4 cup fresh coriander
   leaves, chopped
4 green onions, chopped

Heat the oil in a large wok and sauté the garlic, onion and tofu until light golden brown, stirring frequently and gently to keep the tofu in cubes. Add the mushrooms, leek, rice and sauté for 3 minutes. Add the soy sauce, salt, sesame seeds, and pepper and stir-fry for 2 minutes. Garnish with the coriander leaves and green onions.

Serves 4-6.

STIR-FRIED RICE WITH TOFU

3 tablespoons canola oil
1 small yellow onion, finely
chopped
3 cloves garlic, crushed
1/2 lb. pork loin or chicken
breast, cut into julienne
strips
2 cups tofu puffs, cut into
julienne strips (fried tofu)
1 large carrot, peeled, finely
chopped
1 cup finely chopped string
beans
3 cups cooked white or
brown rice
1 tablespoon ketchup
1 teaspoon salt
1/2 teaspoon ground white
pepper
4 green onions, chopped
1/4 cup fresh coriander
leaves, chopped

Heat the oil in a wok and sauté the onion and garlic until golden brown. Add the pork and sauté for 5 minutes, stirring frequently. Add the tofu puffs, carrot, and string beans and stir-fry for 3 minutes. Add the rice, ketchup, salt, and pepper and stir-fry for 2 minutes. Garnish with the green onions and coriander leaves. Serve hot.

Serves 4-6.

Tofu Risotto

1 cup canola oil for deep-frying
1 pkg. firm tofu (16 oz.), drained, cut into 1/2-inch cubes
3 cups cooked white or brown rice
2 cups Italian Tomato Sauce (see page 16)
1/4 lb. cooked ham, thinly sliced or 1 pkg. chopped frozen spinach (10 oz.), thawed, squeezed dry
1/2 cup Italian parsley, chopped
1/2 cup grated mozzarella cheese
1/2 cup grated Parmesan cheese

Heat the oil in a wok and deep-fry the tofu cubes for 3 minutes or until golden brown on both sides. Remove and drain on paper towels. Set aside. In a buttered 9x13 inch baking pan, arrange alternately the rice, fried tofu, tomato sauce, ham (or spinach), parsley, mozzarella, and Parmesan cheese in layers. Bake in a 350 degree oven for 30 minutes or until the top is brown. Serve hot.

Serves 4-6.

BAKED JUMBO PASTA SHELLS

1 cup soft tofu, drained,
   mashed
2 eggs, beaten
1/2 cup Italian parsley,
   chopped
1/2 teaspoon nutmeg
1 teaspoon fresh basil,
   chopped
1/2 teaspoon salt
1/2 teaspoon ground black
   pepper
2 cups ricotta cheese
1 cup grated mozzarella
   cheese
24 jumbo pasta shells,
   cooked, drained
3 cups Italian Tomato Sauce
   (see page 16)
1/2 cup grated Parmesan
   cheese

In a large bowl, thoroughly mix the tofu, eggs, parsley, nutmeg, basil, salt, pepper, ricotta, and mozzarella cheese. Fill the jumbo pasta shells with the tofu mixture. Place the stuffed jumbo pasta shells in a 9x13 inch baking pan and cover with the Italian Tomato Sauce. Sprinkle with the Parmesan cheese. Bake in a 350 degree oven for 40 minutes.

Serves 4-6.

LASAGNA

2 tablespoons olive oil
4 cloves garlic, crushed
1 small yellow onion,
finely chopped
1 cup frozen spinach,
thawed, squeezed dry,
chopped or 1 cup lean
ground beef
1/2 cup Italian parsley,
chopped
1 teaspoon salt
1/2 teaspoon ground black
pepper
2 cups soft tofu, drained,
mashed
1/2 cup bread crumbs
1 egg, beaten (optional)
1/4 cup ricotta cheese
1/2 cup grated Parmesan
cheese
1 lb. lasagna noodles,
cooked
3 cups Italian Tomato Sauce
(see page 16)
1 1/2 cups grated mozzarella
cheese

Heat the oil in a large pot and sauté the garlic and onion until light golden brown. Add the spinach, parsley, salt and pepper and sauté for 3 minutes. Pour the mixture into a large bowl and thoroughly mix the tofu, bread crumbs, egg, ricotta cheese and 4 tablespoons of grated Parmesan cheese. Set aside. In a buttered and floured 9x13 inch baking pan, arrange the cooked lasagna noodles, tofu and spinach filling, Italian Tomato Sauce and mozzarella cheese in layers. Repeat the process until all the noodles are used, making sure that the top layer is covered by the Italian Tomato Sauce. Sprinkle the top with the remaining Parmesan cheese. Bake in a 350 degree oven for 30 minutes or until the top is brown.

Serves 4-6.

MANICOTTI

3 tablespoons olive oil
1 small yellow onion,
  finely chopped
2 cups firm tofu, drained,
  mashed
4 cloves garlic, crushed
1 teaspoon salt
1 pkg. frozen chopped
  spinach (10 oz.), thawed,
  squeezed dry
1/2 cup Italian parsley,
  finely chopped
1 cup grated mozzarella
  cheese
1 cup ricotta cheese
3 quarts water
1 pkg. large manicotti (8 oz.)
3 cups Italian Tomato Sauce
  (see page 16)
1/4 cup grated Parmesan
  cheese

Heat the oil in a large pot and sauté the onion until light golden brown. Add the tofu, garlic, salt, spinach, and parsley and sauté for 2 minutes. Let it cool, then pour the mixture into a large bowl and mix in the mozzarella and ricotta cheese. Set aside. Bring the water to a boil in a large deep pot, drop in the large manicotti and boil them for 7 minutes or until they are tender. Rinse and drain carefully. Fill each large manicotti with 3 tablespoons of the filling. Place the stuffed large manicotti in a buttered 9x13 inch baking pan and cover them with the Italian Tomato Sauce. Sprinkle with the Parmesan cheese. Bake in a 350 degree oven for 40 minutes.

Serves 4-6.

PESTO SPAGHETTI

1/2 cup Italian parsley,
chopped
3 cups fresh basil leaves,
washed, drained
4 cloves garlic, crushed
1/2 teaspoon salt
1/2 cup soft tofu, drained,
mashed
1/2 cup pine nuts, crushed
3/4 cup grated Parmesan
cheese
1/2 cup olive oil
4 quarts water
1 pkg. thin spaghetti (1 lb.)

In a blender, blend the Italian parsley, basil leaves, garlic, salt and tofu until it is a smooth paste. Pour the paste in a large bowl and add the crushed pine nuts, Parmesan cheese, and olive oil. Stir well and set aside. In a large deep pot, bring the water to a boil. Add the spaghetti and cook uncovered for 8 to 10 minutes, stirring occasionally. Do not overcook the spaghetti. Remove and drain in a colander. Place the spaghetti and pesto paste in a large bowl. Toss very well and serve immediately.

Serves 4-6.

SPAGHETTI WITH TOFU

1 cup milk
1 cup soft tofu, drained
1/2 teaspoon salt
1/4 teaspoon dry mustard
1/2 cup grated Parmesan
cheese
2 tablespoons butter or
olive oil
1 small yellow onion,
finely chopped
3 quarts water
1 pkg. thin spaghetti (1 lb.)

In a blender, blend the milk, tofu, salt, mustard, and Parmesan cheese until smooth. Set aside. Heat the oil in a deep pot and sauté the onion until light golden brown. Add the blended mixture and simmer for 2 minutes. In a large deep pot, bring the water to a boil. Add the spaghetti and cook uncovered for 8 to 10 minutes, stirring occasionally. Do not overcook the spaghetti. Remove and drain in a colander. Place the spaghetti on a large serving platter and pour the sauce over it. Serve hot.

Serves 4-6.

SPINACH TOFU NOODLES

1 pkg. frozen chopped
spinach (10 oz.), thawed,
squeezed dry
1/2 cup soft tofu, drained
2 tablespoons olive oil
1/4 teaspoon salt
2 to 2 1/4 cups flour

In a blender, blend the spinach, tofu, oil, and salt until smooth and creamy. Pour the tofu mixture in a large bowl and add the flour. Mix and knead for 5 minutes or until smooth and soft. Put through a pasta machine or roll out by hand. Cut to desired size. Boil in water for 5 minutes and serve with Italian Tomato Sauce (see page 16), or White Clam Sauce (see page 20).

Serves 4.

TOFU CHOW MEIN

3 tablespoons canola oil
3 cloves garlic, crushed
1 small yellow onion,
　finely chopped
1 large carrot, peeled, cut
　into julienne strips
1 cup fresh mushrooms,
　washed, drained, thinly
　sliced
1 fresh red cayenne pepper,
　sliced (optional)
1 pkg. extra firm tofu
　(12.4 oz.), drained, cubed
1 cup snow pea pods, ends
　removed
1 lb. noodles, cooked
1 cup fresh bean sprouts
1 teaspoon brown sugar
2 tablespoons soy sauce
2 tablespoons soy bean
　paste (Brown Rice Miso),
　dissolved in a 1/4 cup
　warm water
4 green onions, chopped
1/4 cup fresh coriander
　leaves, chopped

Heat the oil in a large wok and sauté the garlic and onion until light golden brown. Add the carrot, mushrooms, cayenne pepper, tofu, and pea pods and stir-fry for 3 minutes. Add the noodles, bean sprouts, sugar, soy sauce, and miso mixture and stir-fry for 2 minutes or until well-mixed. Garnish with the green onions and coriander leaves.

Serves 4-6.

TOFU NOODLES

1 cup soft tofu, drained
2 tablespoons olive oil
1/2 teaspoon salt
2 cups flour

In a blender, blend the tofu, oil, and salt until smooth and creamy. Pour the tofu mixture into a large bowl and add the flour. Mix and knead for 5 minutes or until smooth and soft. Put the dough through a pasta machine or roll it out by hand. Cut to desired size. Boil in water for 5 minutes and serve with Italian Tomato Sauce (see page 16), and Tofu Meat Balls (see page 106).

Serves 4.

TOFU TOMATO NOODLES

1 cup soft tofu, drained
2 tablespoons olive oil
1/4 cup tomato paste
2 cups flour

In a blender, blend the tofu, oil, and tomato paste until smooth and creamy. Pour the tofu mixture into a large bowl and add the flour. Mix and knead for 5 minutes or until smooth and soft. Put it through a pasta machine or roll it out by hand. Cut to desired size. Boil in water for 5 minutes and serve with Italian Tomato Sauce (see page 16), and Tofu Meat Balls (see page 106) or White Clam Sauce (see page 20).

Serves 4.

CHAPTER NINE

DESSERTS

Desserts

APPLE CAKE

2 cups flour, sifted
2 teaspoons baking powder
1/2 teaspoon baking soda
2 teaspoons ground
cinnamon
1 1/4 cups brown sugar
1/2 cup canola oil
2 eggs, beaten
1 cup soft tofu, drained,
mashed
2 cups shredded apples
1 cup walnuts, chopped

In a large bowl, mix the flour, baking powder and baking soda. Set aside. In another bowl, mix the cinnamon, sugar, oil, eggs, and tofu. Add the tofu mixture to the flour mixture along with the apples and walnuts. Stir all the ingredients until just blended. Pour the batter into a buttered and floured 9x13 inch baking pan. Bake in a 350 degree oven for 40 minutes or until the cake is done. Let cool before serving.

Serves 6-8.

APPLE PUDDING

4 cups shredded apples
1/4 cup brown sugar
1/2 cup soft tofu, drained,
mashed
1/4 cup whipping cream
2 cups crushed graham
crackers

In a large bowl, mix the apples and sugar, then spread the apple mixture evenly on a cookie sheet. Bake in a 350 degree oven for 5 minutes. Set aside and cool. In a 9x13 inch baking pan, arrange the apple mixture, tofu, whipping cream and graham crackers in layers. Refrigerate overnight before serving.

Serves 6-8.

CARROT CAKE

2 cups flour
2 teaspoons baking powder
1 1/2 teaspoons baking soda
1/2 teaspoon salt
2 teaspoons ground
  cinnamon
1 3/4 cups brown sugar
1 cup canola oil
2 eggs, beaten
1 teaspoon vanilla
2 cups fresh shredded
  carrots
1/2 cup soft tofu, drained,
  mashed
1 cup raisins
1 cup flaked coconut
1 cup chopped walnuts
1 can pineapple (8 1/4 oz.),
  crushed, drained

In a large bowl, sift the flour, baking powder, baking soda, salt, and cinnamon. Add the sugar, oil, eggs, and vanilla. Mix well with a wooden spoon until smooth. Add the carrots, tofu, raisins, coconut, walnuts, and pineapple and stir until well-blended. Pour the mixture into a buttered and floured 9x13 inch baking pan. Bake in a 350 degree oven for 45 minutes or until the cake is done. Cool before frosting. Frost with Tofu Cream Cheese Frosting (see page 142).

Serves 6-8.

CHEESE CAKE

2 cups graham crackers,
  finely crushed
2 tablespoons honey
1/4 cup butter or margarine,
  melted
2 tablespoons unflavored
  gelatine
1/4 cup cold water
1/3 cup sugar
1 cup soft tofu, drained,
  mashed
1 1/2 cups yogurt
1 pkg. cream cheese (3 oz.)
2 tablespoons fresh orange
  juice

In a bowl, mix the crushed graham crackers, honey and butter with your fingers until well-blended. Press the crumb mixture into a 9-inch pie pan. Bake in a 350 degree oven for 5 minutes. Cool the crust before filling. In a small pot, add the gelatine and water and stir it over low heat until the gelatine is completely dissolved. Set aside. In a blender, blend the sugar, tofu, yogurt, cream cheese and orange juice until smooth. Add the melted gelatine and blend until smooth. Pour the mixture into the crumb pie shell. Refrigerate 5 hours or overnight. Before serving, garnish with any kind of fresh fruit.

Serves 4-6.

CHOCOLATE CHIP COOKIES

1 1/2 cups flour
3/4 teaspoon baking
  powder
1 cup chocolate chips
1/2 cup walnuts, chopped
3/4 cup brown sugar
1/2 cup canola oil
1/2 cup soft tofu, drained,
  mashed
1 egg, beaten (optional)
1 teaspoon vanilla

In a large bowl, mix the flour, baking powder, chocolate chips, and walnuts. Set aside. With an electric mixer, beat the sugar, oil, tofu, egg, and vanilla into a smooth and creamy paste. Pour the mixture into the bowl with the dry ingredients and mix well with a wooden spoon. Drop the mixture by spoonfuls onto oiled cookie sheets. Bake in a 400 degree oven for 10 to 15 minutes or until light golden brown.

Makes 14 cookies.

CHOCOLATE COFFEE COOKIES

1 1/2 cups flour
3/4 teaspoon baking powder
1/2 cup chocolate powder
2 tablespoons instant coffee
  powder
3/4 cup brown sugar
1/2 cup canola oil
1/2 cup soft tofu, drained,
  mashed

In a large bowl, mix the flour, baking powder, chocolate, and coffee powder. Set aside. With an electric mixer, beat the sugar, oil and tofu into a smooth and creamy paste. Pour the mixture into the dry ingredients and mix well with a wooden spoon. Drop the mixture by spoonfuls onto oiled cookie sheets. Bake in a 400 degree oven for 10 to 15 minutes or until light golden brown.

Makes 14 cookies.

COCONUT TOFU COOKIES

1 1/2 cups flour
3/4 teaspoon baking powder
1/4 teaspoon salt
1 cup shredded coconut
1/2 cup walnuts, chopped
3/4 cup sugar
1/2 cup canola oil
1/2 cup soft tofu, drained,
  mashed
1 teaspoon vanilla

In a large bowl, mix the flour, baking powder, salt, coconut, and walnuts. With an electric mixer, beat the sugar, oil, tofu and vanilla into a smooth and creamy paste. Pour the mixture into the bowl with the dry ingredients and mix well with a wooden spoon. Drop the mixture by spoonfuls onto oiled cookie sheets. Bake in a 400 degree oven for 10 to 15 minutes or until light golden brown.

Makes 14 cookies.

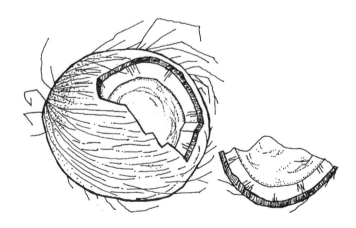

MANGO CREAM PIE

2 1/2 cups flour
3/4 cup butter or margarine
3 tablespoons cold water
3/4 cup sugar
2 large ripe mangoes,
  peeled, seeded
1 cup soft tofu, drained,
  mashed
2 eggs, separated
2 tablespoons fresh orange
  juice
2/3 cup whipping cream
2 tablespoons unflavored
  gelatine
1/2 cup warm water

In a bowl, thoroughly mix the flour, butter and water into a crumbly dough. Press the dough into a 10-inch pie pan, using your fingers, or roll the dough out between 2 pieces of wax paper. Transfer the dough to a pie pan. Bake in a 350 degree oven for 20 minutes or until the pie crust is light brown. Cool the pie crust before filling it. In a blender, blend the sugar, mangoes, tofu, egg yolks, and orange juice until smooth. Mix in the whipping cream and set aside. In a small pot, combine the gelatine and warm water. Stir until the gelatine is dissolved. Pour into a bowl and add the mango mixture and stir until blended. Stiffly beat the egg whites and gently fold them into the mango mixture. Pour the mango cream filling into a baked pie crust. Chill for 2 hours or overnight in a refrigerator before serving.

Serves 4-6.

ORANGE WAFFLES

1 3/4 cups flour
2 teaspoons baking powder
1/4 teaspoon salt
1/4 teaspoon nutmeg
1/2 cup soft tofu, drained,
   mashed
1 teaspoon fresh, grated
   orange peel
3/4 cup milk or soy bean
   milk (see page 146)
1 tablespoon honey
1/3 cup melted butter or
   margarine
3 eggs, separated

In a large bowl, combine the flour, baking powder, salt, and nutmeg. Set aside. In another bowl, mix the tofu, orange peel, milk, honey, butter, and yolks until very smooth. Add the flour mixture and mix until evenly blended. Stiffly beat the egg whites and gently fold them into the mixture. Bake on a heated waffle iron. Serve with fresh fruit and Tofu Almond Whip (see page143).

Serves 4-6.

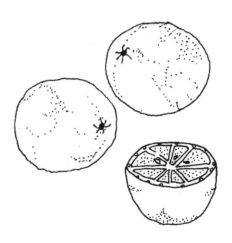

POPPY SEED CAKE

1 cup soft tofu, drained,
   mashed
2/3 cup sugar
1/2 cup canola oil
1 tablespoon baking powder
1/4 teaspoon baking soda
1 egg, beaten (optional)
1 teaspoon vanilla
1/2 cup plain bread crumbs
1 cup fresh orange juice
2 1/2 cups flour
1/4 cup poppy seeds

In a blender, blend the tofu, sugar, oil, baking powder, baking soda, egg, vanilla, and bread crumbs until thoroughly mixed. Pour the mixture into a large bowl and add the orange juice and flour alternately. Add the poppy seeds and mix well. Pour it into a buttered and floured 9x13 inch baking pan. Bake in a 350 degree oven for 45 minutes or until the cake is done. Cool before serving. Serve with Tofu Almond Whip (see page 143).

Serves 6-8.

Pumpkin Chiffon Pie

2 cups flour
3/4 cup butter or margarine
1/2 cup walnuts, crushed
3 tablespoons cold water
3/4 cup brown sugar
1/2 teaspoon salt
2 teaspoons ground
cinnamon
1/2 teaspoon ground ginger
1/2 teaspoon allspice
1 cup pumpkin, cooked,
mashed
1/2 cup soft tofu, drained,
mashed
1/2 cup milk or soy bean
milk (see page 146)
3 large eggs, separated
1 teaspoon brandy
1/2 teaspoon fresh, finely
grated orange peel
2 tablespoons unflavored
gelatine
1/2 cup warm water

In a large bowl, thoroughly mix the flour, butter, walnuts, and water into a crumbly dough. Press the dough into a 10-inch pie pan, using your fingers, or roll the dough out between 2 pieces of wax paper, and transfer it to a pie pan. Bake in a 350 degree oven for 20 minutes or until the pie crust is light brown. Cool the pie crust before filling. In a large deep pot, combine the sugar, salt, cinnamon, ginger, allspice, pumpkin, tofu, milk, egg yolks, brandy, and orange peel. Stir and simmer for 5 minutes. Set aside. In a small pot, combine the gelatine and warm water. Stir well until the gelatine is dissolved, then pour it into a large bowl, add the pumpkin mixture, and stir until well-blended. Stiffly beat the egg whites and gently fold them into the pumpkin mixture. Pour the pumpkin mixture into the baked pie crust and chill for 4 hours or overnight in a refrigerator. Serve with Tofu Whip (see page 143).

Serves 4-6.

RASPBERRY CHIFFON PIE

2 cups flour
3/4 cup butter or margarine
1/2 cup walnuts, finely
  crushed
3 tablespoons cold water
1 cup fresh raspberries
1/2 cup soy bean milk
  (see page146) or
  regular milk
1/2 cup soft tofu, drained,
  mashed
1/3 cup honey
3 eggs, separated
1 tablespoon unflavored
  gelatine
1/4 cup warm water
1 pint whipping cream
1/2 cup raspberries for
  garnish

In a large bowl, thoroughly mix the flour, butter, walnuts, and water into a crumbly dough. Press the dough into a 10-inch pie pan using your fingers, or roll the dough out between 2 pieces of wax paper and transfer it to a pie pan. Bake in a 350 degree oven for 20 minutes or until the pie crust is lightly browned. Cool the pie crust before filling it. In a blender, blend the raspberries, soy milk, tofu, honey, and yolks until very smooth. Set aside. In a small pot, combine the gelatine and warm water. Stir well until the gelatine is dissolved, then blend it into the raspberry mixture. Whip the whipping cream until stiff. Fold the whipped cream into the raspberry mixture. Stiffly beat the egg whites and fold them into the raspberry mixture. Pour the mixture into the baked pie crust and chill for 4 hours or overnight in a refrigerator. Garnish with the 1/2 cup of raspberries.

Serves 4-6.

STRAWBERRY TOFU ICE CREAM

1 cup soft tofu, drained, mashed 1 pint whipping cream 1 cup milk or soy bean milk (see page 146) 1 cup sugar 2 pkgs. frozen unsweetened strawberries	In a large bowl, mix the tofu, whipping cream, milk, sugar, and strawberries. Put the mixture into an ice cream maker or place the mixture in a pan in the freezer and freeze it until it is icy and almost set. Scrape it into a mixing bowl and beat it thoroughly with a wooden spoon, or at low speed with an electric mixer. Return it to the freezer and freeze it until it is set.

Serves 4.

TOFU BROWNIES

2/3 cup flour, sifted 1 teaspoon baking powder 2 eggs, beaten 1/2 cup sugar or honey 1/2 cup butter or margarine, melted 1/2 cup unsweetened cocoa powder 1/2 cup soft tofu, drained, mashed 1 teaspoon vanilla 1/2 cup chopped walnuts	In a small bowl, mix the flour and baking powder. Set aside. In a large bowl, beat the eggs, sugar, butter, cocoa powder, tofu, and vanilla until well-blended. Add the flour mixture and mix well. Stir in the nuts. Pour the mixture into a buttered and floured 8x8 baking pan and bake in a 350 degree oven for 25-30 minutes.

Serves 4-6.

TOFU CREAM CHEESE FROSTING

1/3 cup butter or margarine
2 cups powdered sugar
1/3 cup cream cheese
1/3 cup soft tofu, drained,
  mashed
1 tablespoon fresh lime juice
1 teaspoon vanilla

With an electric mixer, beat the butter, sugar, cream cheese, tofu, lime juice, and vanilla until smooth and creamy. Refrigerate before using.

Makes 2 cups.

TOFU FUDGE

1/2 cup soft tofu, drained,
  mashed
1 teaspoon vanilla
1/2 cup cocoa powder
1/4 teaspoon salt
2 tablespoons butter or
  margarine, melted
2/3 cup sugar
1 teaspoon baking powder
1/2 cup flour
2/3 cup walnuts, chopped

In a blender, blend the tofu, vanilla, cocoa powder, salt, butter, and sugar until smooth. Pour the mixture into a bowl and add the baking powder, flour and walnuts and stir all the ingredients until well-mixed. Pour into a buttered 8x10 inch baking pan. Bake in a 350 degree oven for 30 minutes or until the fudge is done. Cool and cut into small squares.

Serves 4-6.

TOFU WHIP

1 cup soft tofu, drained, mashed
3 tablespoons canola oil
3 tablespoons powdered sugar
1 teaspoon vanilla
1 teaspoon fresh lime juice

In a blender, mix all the ingredients until smooth. Cover and refrigerate before using. To be used in place of whipped cream.

Makes 1 cup.

TOFU ALMOND WHIP

1 cup soft tofu, drained, mashed
3 tablespoons canola oil
3 tablespoons powdered sugar
1 teaspoon almond extract

In a blender, mix all the ingredients until smooth. Cover and refrigerate before using. To be used in place of whipped cream.

Makes 1 cup.

YOGURT CAKE

Dough

1 1/4 cups plain yogurt
1/4 cup soft tofu, drained,
  mashed
2 1/4 cups sugar
3 eggs, well-beaten
1/4 cup butter or margarine,
  melted
3 cups flour, sifted
1 teaspoon baking soda

Orange Syrup

1/2 cup sugar
2 teaspoons fresh, grated
  orange peel
1 teaspoon fresh, grated
  lemon peel
3 cups fresh orange juice

With an electric mixer, beat the yogurt, tofu, and sugar for a few seconds. Consecutively add and beaten eggs, melted butter, flour, and baking soda until very smooth. Pour into a buttered 9x13 inch baking pan. Bake in a 375 degree oven for 30-40 minutes or until the cake is done. Cool and cut into squares. Set aside. In a small pot, bring the sugar, orange peel, lemon peel, and orange juice to a boil for 5 minutes. Remove from heat. Let cool. With a large wooden spoon, slowly pour the orange syrup over the cake. Chill overnight in a refrigerator before serving.

Serves 8-10.

CHOCOLATE TOFU SHAKE

1 cup soft tofu, drained
1 cup milk or soy bean milk
(see page146)
1 teaspoon fresh orange
juice
1 tablespoon sugar
3 teaspoons cocoa
1/4 teaspoon ground
cinnamon

In a blender, blend the tofu, milk, orange juice, sugar, cocoa and cinnamon until very smooth. Chill in a refrigerator before serving.

Serves 2.

KAHLUA SHAKE

1 cup soft tofu, drained
1 cup strong coffee
1 tablespoon cocoa powder
2 tablespoons sugar
1 teaspoon vanilla
3 tablespoons kahlua

In a blender, blend the tofu, coffee, cocoa, sugar, vanilla, and kahlua until very smooth. Chill in a refrigerator before serving.

Serves 2.

STRAWBERRY TOFU SHAKE

1 cup soft tofu, drained
1 cup milk or soy bean milk
(see page 146)
1/2 cup fresh strawberries,
washed, drained
2 tablespoons sugar
1 teaspoon vanilla

In a blender, blend the tofu, milk, strawberries, sugar, and vanilla until very smooth. Chill in a refrigerator before serving.

Serves 2.

SOY BEAN MILK

1 cup whole dried soy beans,
washed, soaked overnight,
drained
4 cups water

In a blender, blend the soy beans with water until it is a smooth paste. Line a colander with a cheese cloth and place it in a large deep pot. Pour the blended mixture into the cloth-lined colander. Allow the mixture to strain through the cheese cloth. Next, gather the 4 corners of the cheese cloth and squeeze out the remaining liquid. (Either discard the remaining pulp or add it to cookie dough, meat loaf, stuffing, etc.) Bring the soy bean milk to a boil and cook it over low heat for 3 minutes, uncovered. Serve hot or cold.

Makes 4 cups.

Cleaning and Scoring Squid

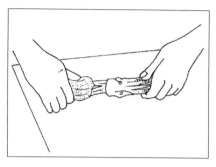

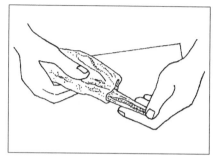

1. Pull the tentacles from the body of the squid; the intestines will also come out.

2. Pull out the quill from the body.

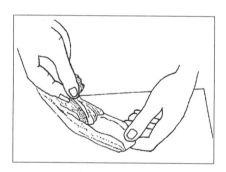

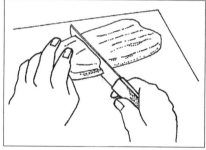

3. Peel off the outer skin, rinse out the body and cut the tentacles off at the head.

4. Cut to size, depending on the recipe.

Filling and Wrapping Wontons

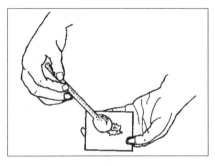

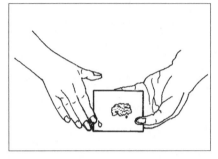

1. Place one teaspoonful on the pork mixture in the center of the wrapper.

2. Wet the edges of the wrapper.

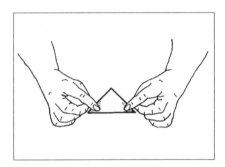

3. Fold it up into a triangle by pinching the three corners together.

4. Wet one of the bottom corners of the triangle and fold it over to overlap the opposite corner and join them by pinching them together.

Shelling and Deveining Shrimp

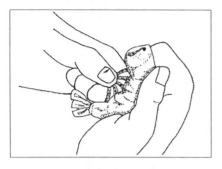

1. From the underside of shrimp, remove the legs.

2. Roll back the shell from the underside, removing or keeping the tail, as desired.

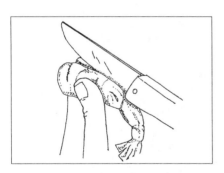

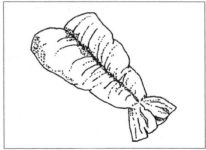

3. To devein, cut along the back (not completely through) and remove the vein.

4. If butterflying is desired, cut deeper along the back and spread the halves open along the cut in the back.

Suggested Menus

These suggested menus show that tofu and other soyfood meals can be healthy, nutritious, light, simple or even elegant for your every day use. Below are listed some menu suggestions which can be enjoyed by you, your family and guests. Try them and enjoy.

Vegetarian Menus

Beet and Potato Salad, page 59
Hot Sweet Sauce, page 15
Barbecued Tofu with Vegetables, page 29

Fennel Salad, page 61
Stuffed Mushrooms, page 33
Eggplant Lasagna, page 71

Tahini Tofu Dip, page 27
Lebanese Salad, page 62
Stuffed Baked Tomatoes, page 78

Hot Curry Dip, page 25
Lentil Salad, page 63
Stuffed Eggplant, page 79

Borscht, page 39
Meatless Tofu Balls, page 72
Stuffed Zucchini, page 80

Creamy Leek Soup, page 42
Tofu Spanakopita, page 35
Tofu Ratatouille, page 83

Hearty Vegetable Soup, page 44
Tofuburgers with Yuba, page 81
Tartar Sauce, page 19

Elegant Menus

Crab Spread, page 24
Corn and Shrimp Soup, page 40
Mandarin Orange Salad, page 64
Stir-Fried Shrimp and Squid, page 97
Chicken with Cashew Nuts, page 116
Strawberry Tofu Ice Cream, page 141

Tofu with Jamaican Jerk Sauce, page 36
Creamy Eggplant Soup, page 41
Seafood Salad with Tofu, page 65
Tofu and Beef with Basil, page 105
Stuffed Tofu, page 114
Apple Pudding, page 131

Mushroom Dip, page 25
Minestrone Soup, page 46
Stir-Fried Yuba with Tofu, page 77
Crab Soufflé, page 91
Yogurt Cake, page 144

Salmon Spread, page 26
Spicy Sweet and Sour Soup, page 51
Stuffed Nori with Crab, page 92
Spicy Sweet and Sour Tofu Balls, page 74
Black Beans with Pork and Tofu, page 110
Poppy Seed Cake, page 138

Tofu Satay, page 34
Spicy Prawn Soup, page 50
Spicy Thai Mixed Vegetables, page 75
Vegetables with Spicy Peanut Sauce, page 88
Pumpkin Chiffon Pie, page 139

Glossary

ASAFOETIDIA: (Hing) A strong, sulfurous aromatic spice; basically a gum extract from a tree. It is widely used in Indian cooking, particularly with dal, as it is an anti-flatulent. Keep in a tightly closed jar. Available in Indian and Pakistani groceries.

BABY CORN: Miniature ears of corn, available in cans in Asian markets.

BAMBOO SHOOTS: A crisp, cream-colored, conical-shaped vegetable used frequently in all Asian cooking. It is much simpler to buy the canned variety which is readily available in all Asian and many Western markets.

BLACK CHINESE MUSHROOMS: Although sold dried, they must be soaked in warm water for some time before using. The hard stems are discarded. Available in Asian and Western markets.

CAPERS: Small, green, pickled buds of a Mediterranean flowering plant; usually packed in brine. Available in the gourmet food sections of supermarkets.

CAYENNE PEPPERS: Very hot peppers, available fresh or dried in most markets.

CELLOPHANE NOODLES: Also known as "bean thread vermicelli", a firm transparent noodle made from mung beans. They are usually soaked in warm water for 5 minutes before use. They are also deep-fried straight from the packet when used as a garnish.

COCONUT MILK: Made by combining freshly grated coconut with water, then squeezing and straining. Available in cans or powdered in most markets. No substitute.

CUMIN: The most essential ingredient in the preparation of curry, it is available in seed form or ground.

DILL WEED: An aromatic, annual herb whose leaves and seeds are used as a seasoning for fish, pickles, dips, etc. Available in most markets.

FENNEL BULB: Its overlapping stems look almost like a bulb and its feathery green tops are used like an herb, for sprinkling. The bulb is used raw in salads. Available in gourmet food sections of supermarkets.

FENNEL SEEDS: An aromatic seed used as flavoring. Available in Asian and Western markets.

FILO LEAVES OR FILO DOUGH: (also spelled Phyllo) Paper thin pastry of Middle Eastern origin. Besides its Greek name above, it may also be called brik, yukka, or malsouka. Because it takes great skill and patience to make filo, many people prefer to buy it frozen. It can be purchased in 1/2 lb. and 1 lb. packages in the gourmet food sections of supermarkets or Middle Eastern groceries.

FISH SAUCE: A thin, salty, brown sauce used in Southeast Asian cooking to bring out the flavor in food. Available in Asian and Western markets.

FRESH CORIANDER: Also known as cilantro and Chinese parsley, it has a very distinctive flavor. It is available in seed form or ground in most markets. No substitute.

FRESH MINT: There are many varieties; however, the common round-leafed mint (Spearmint) is the one most often used.

GARAM MASALA: A mixture of spices which can either be made up at home from freshly ground spices or bought ready-made. A basic mixture contains cumin, ground black pepper, cloves, cinnamon and cardamom.

GINGER: A smooth-skinned, buff-colored root, used both for seasoning dishes and as a condiment.

ITALIAN PARSLEY: Broad leafed parsley, available in most markets.

JAPANESE EGGPLANT: Four to six inches long and about two inches in diameter, this eggplant is very tasty and tender. Available in Asian and Western markets.

KAFFIR LIME LEAVES: (Fragrant Lime Leaves) An aromatic type of leaf with a strong lime fragrance. Grated lime peel can be used as a poor substitute. They are sold fresh, frozen or dried in Asian markets.

LAOS ROOT: (Galangal) Delicate in flavor with brown skin and creamy white flesh, it is sold in powdered form or as a dried root in Asian markets.

LEMON GRASS: An aromatic type of grass with a strong lemony fragrance, also known as "serah", it grows with a small bulbous root. No substitute. It is sold fresh, powdered, chopped, or in dried slices in Asian markets.

NORI: (Seaweed sheets) It is conveniently prepared in the form of paper-thin, purplish-black sheets, each about 8 inches square and ready to add to dishes without cooking. It is used in soups, salads or as a garnish. It is rich in minerals and available in Asian, health and natural food markets.

OYSTER SAUCE: Made from oysters cooked in salted water and soy sauce. It keeps well and adds a delicate flavor to meat and vegetable dishes.

PINE NUTS: (Pinoli or Pignoli) Extracted from the huge cones of the umbrella pine, these slender cream-colored little nuts have a unique flavor, are slightly aromatic and rich. Available in the gourmet food sections of most supermarkets.

SALTED BLACK BEANS: A highly flavorful ingredient made from black soy beans which have been cooked and fermented. Used to season meat, chicken and seafood. Available in Asian stores in cans or plastic bags.

SESAME OIL: Extracted from toasted sesame seeds, it is widely used in Chinese and Korean cooking in small quantities for flavoring. Available in Asian and Western markets.

SESAME SEEDS: Small flat seeds used as a source of oil and as a garnish. Available in Asian and Western markets.

SOY BEAN MILK: A nutty milk extracted from soy beans with water, it is curdled to make tofu and available in Asian and most fancy grade food stores.

SOY BEAN PASTE: (Miso) A paste of fermented soy beans, cereal grain and sea salt. Available in Asian markets and in the gourmet food sections of supermarkets.

SOY SAUCE: (Shoyu) A sauce made by fermenting soy beans and wheat in water.

STRAW MUSHROOMS: Usually canned, they have a delicate flavor and chewy texture. Available in Asian markets.

STRIP KOMBU SEAWEED: A sea vegetable rich in minerals. Sold in olive-brown strands which can be cut with scissors and used in making vegetable soup and stew broths. Available in Asian, health and natural food stores.

TAHINI: (Sesame Paste) A Middle Eastern paste made from crushed sesame seeds and used mainly for its creamy, rich and nutty flavor as well as for binding sauces together.

TOFU PUFFS: (Fried Tofu) Also known as age or aburage, age puffs, fried soy bean cakes, or tofu pouches. These deep-fried pouches can be split open and stuffed with vegetables, or cut into thin strips and used in salads, soups, stews and casseroles. They are high in protein and have a chewy and meat-like texture. Available in Asian stores.

TOFU: (Soy Bean Curd) A soft white curd which is made from soy beans and resembles fresh white cheese. It is bland, having little taste of its own, but taking on the flavor of whatever it is cooked with. It is high in protein and low in calories; it is low in saturated fat and is cholesterol-free. It is also rich in vitamins and minerals. Four kinds of Tofu are widely available (Soft, Medium, Firm, and Extra Firm) which are sold in little plastic containers that are sealed so that you can look through the top. Each container of tofu weighs 10 to 16 ounces. Available in Asian and Western markets.

WATER CHESTNUTS: Usually canned, but occasionally found fresh, water chestnuts have a crunchy texture. When fresh, their brown skin must be peeled off with a sharp knife and discarded.

WHITE ICICLE RADISH: (Daikon) A long white, sweet radish native to Japan, it is often served grated with deep-fried, oily foods, as it is considered an aid to digestion. Available in Asian and health food stores.

WHITE LENTILS: (Urad Dal) Similar in shape and size to mung beans, this dal is white and a little drier when cooked. It is popular among Northern Indians. It can be found in Indian and Pakistani groceries.

YUBA STICKS: (Dry Bean Curd) A nutritious and very high proteined soy food, made by drying out the skin that forms when cooking soy milk. Available in Asian markets.

Index

Truly **Ambrosia**

Delightful Tofu Cooking

Delightful Vietnamese Cooking

Delightful Brazilian Cooking

Delightful Thai Cooking

coming soon

Delightful Chinese Cooking

Delightful Indonesian Cooking

Delightful Italian Cooking

Ordering Information

Please send me:

___copies of Delightful Tofu Cooking, $12.95 each $_____
___copies of Delightful Vietnamese Cooking, $12.95 each $_____
___copies of Delightful Brazilian Cooking, $14.95 each $_____
___copies of Delightful Thai Cooking, $10.95 each $_____
___set of 4 copies, $40.00 a set $_____

Shipping & Handling:
              $3.00   1st copy $_____
              $1.00   each additional copy $_____
              $6.00   set of 4 $_____
Washington State residents add 8.2% sales tax. $_____

                       Total Enclosed $_____

Payment:

❑ Check   ❑ Money Order

Mail Payment To:

Ambrosia Publications
P.O. Box 30818
Seattle, WA 98103
Phone (206) 789-3693
Fax (206) 789- 3693

Ship Order To:

Name _____
Address _____
City _____
State _____ Zip Code _____
❑Autographed by the author ? To whom ?_____